DEAN F. OLIVER | LAURA BRANDON | FOREWORD BY J. L. GRANATSTEIN

CANVAS OF WAR

PAINTING THE CANADIAN EXPERIENCE | 1914 TO 1945

Douglas & McIntyre

Vancouver/Toronto

Canadian War Museum

Ottawa

Canadian Museum of
Civilization Corporation

Hull

Copyright © 2000 by Canadian War Museum/
Canadian Museum of Civilization Corporation

First paperback edition 2001
01 02 03 04 05   5 4 3 2 1

Douglas & McIntyre Ltd.
2323 Quebec Street, Suite 201
Vancouver, British Columbia V5T 4S7

Cet ouvrage a été publié simultanément en français sous le titre *Tableaux de guerre: Reflets de l'expérience canadienne / 1914 à 1945*.

Canadian Cataloguing in Publication Data
Oliver, Dean Frederick, 1965–
    Canvas of War

    Includes bibliographical references.
    ISBN 1–55054–772–0 (bound)
    ISBN 1–55054–883–2

    1. World War, 1914–1918—Art and the war.
2. World War, 1939–1945—Art and the war. 3. Painting, Canadian. 4. Painting, Modern—20th century—Canada.
I. Brandon, Laura, 1951– II. Title
D810.A7044 2000   758'99404'0971   C99–911329–1

Edited by Lucy Kenward
Jacket and text design by Peter Cocking
Maps by Stuart Daniel/Starshell Maps

Front cover painting by Lawren P. Harris, *Reinforcements Moving up in the Ortona Salient*, 1946: Oil on canvas, 76.3 × 102.1 cm, Canadian War Museum 12712
Frontispiece: detail from Eric Aldwinckle, *Invasion Pattern Normandy*, c. 1945: Oil on canvas, 85.4 × 85.7 cm, Canadian War Museum 10679

Printed and bound in Canada by Friesens
Printed on acid-free paper ∞

We gratefully acknowledge the financial support of the Canada Council for the Arts, the British Columbia Ministry of Tourism, Small Business and Culture, and the Government of Canada through the Book Publishing Industry Development Program (BPIDP) for our publishing activities.

All dimensions of works of art are given height preceding width.

Donald C. Mackay (1906–1979)
Signal Flag Hoist, c. 1945
Oil on canvas
76.1 × 61.0 cm · CWM 10443

Donald C. Mackay joined the Royal Canadian Naval Volunteer Reserve on September 5, 1939. Seven weeks later, inspired by the example of the Halifax-based First World War artist Arthur Lismer, he wrote to H. O. McCurry, director of the National Gallery, enquiring as to whether a Canadian war art scheme would be initiated.

McCurry replied: "I am interested to learn that you are in the Navy and that you are anxious to do something regarding war records. I have had several similar letters from artists throughout the country and I am to-day [October 24, 1939] referring all of them, including yours, to the Department of Defence. I hope that something will be done in this direction, and I will let you know if I hear of anything." On February 16, 1943, Mackay was appointed an official war artist attached to the navy.

ACKNOWLEDGEMENTS

THE AUTHORS OWE a great debt to past and present staff, volunteers and contract workers for the Canadian War Museum who contributed in so many ways to this final volume. Several conservators—especially Danielle Allard, Rebecca Renner and Anita Henry—have ensured that the works reproduced here survive in good repair in order to speak to future generations of Canadians.

Leslie Redman, technical services coordinator, and Bill Kent, the museum's photographer, deserve special mention for their forbearance and responsiveness, as do Corrina Clement and Judy Howard. Cameron Pulsifer and Serge Durflinger, museum historians, edited several drafts of the text with patience and enthusiasm. Liliane Reid-Lafleur and Margo Weiss ensured a constant flow of books and manuscripts to our desks. Archivist Carol Reid and researcher John MacFarlane surveyed the museum's little-known primary collections, and Mike Bechthold researched the maps. Daniel Glenney, the director of programs and collections, made his staff and resources available at every turn to assist.

The Canadian Museum of Civilization, the Canadian War Museum's parent organization, provided administrative and financial support, including the professional services of Tony Glen, a tireless and good-humoured project manager; Harry Foster, photographer; and Deborah Brownrigg, image and printing coordinator. Contractor Wendy McPeake was indefatigable on our behalf, while Lucy Kenward, our editor, was fast, thorough and collegial, a rare combination.

J. L. Granatstein, the war museum's director and chief executive officer (1998–2000), made the project a reality by his faith both in the war art collection and in the authors. He pressed donors for funds, and the Donner Canadian Foundation generously responded. Having the editorial assistance in-house of Canada's most prolific military historian was an enormous advantage. Roger Sarty, director of historical research and exhibit development, was the book's *éminence grise* and responsible overall for the entire war art project. His encyclopedic knowledge of Canada's military past saved the authors from untold errors of fact and interpretation.

Several institutions provided essential professional support. The National Gallery of Canada Library and Archives (Cyndie Campbell and Michael Williams), the National Archives of Canada (Anne Goddard, Paul Marsden and Peter Robertson) and the Imperial War Museum's Art Department, London (Jenny Wood), deserve special thanks.

Finally, we must thank the veterans. In reviewing the histories, memoirs and images of Canada's world wars, we were reminded at every turn of the sacrifices made by ordinary Canadians many years ago on our behalf. We hope to have captured enough of their lives, stories and memories here to help preserve a legacy that those who have not experienced war first-hand will never completely comprehend. We are deeply grateful for the opportunity.

MESSAGE FROM THE MINISTER OF CANADIAN HERITAGE

During the two world wars, men and women paid the price of freedom with their lives. The Canadian War Museum's exhibition *Canvas of War*, the largest exhibition of military art ever organized in Canada, highlights our participation in these two world conflicts and reminds us how important it is to redouble our efforts to promote peace and democracy at home and around the world. The sculptures and paintings, including works by members of the Group of Seven, take us on an emotional journey through history to the fields of battle, where many of our soldiers proved their bravery.

The experiences of war, recorded as historical works and engraved in the memories of those who lived through them, today capture our attention as we see them through the eyes and sensitive interpretation of our artists. As Minister of Canadian Heritage, I am proud to be associated with the publication of this book, which will help to immortalize significant periods of our history. I have every confidence that this work will be a rich source of pride and inspiration.

SHEILA COPPS

MESSAGE FROM THE MINISTER OF VETERANS AFFAIRS

Canadian veterans have left this country an invaluable legacy of valour, patriotism and self sacrifice. As the new Minister of Veterans Affairs, I am daily learning more about our veterans' remarkable achievements. At the same time, I am becoming more aware of the importance of telling their story, illuminating their experiences, and honouring their memory. Our nation's wealth of war art—evocative, insightful and devastatingly honest—helps us visualize the unimaginable horrors of war, placing our veterans' experiences in perspective for posterity.

Veterans Affairs Canada is honoured to be associated with the Canadian War Museum in the production of this book, *Canvas of War*. Through it, I hope that many Canadians will acquire a new respect for our veterans, and a renewed sense of pride in their nation-building achievements. Most importantly, I hope that it will serve as a fitting tribute to the fallen. *Lest we forget.*

GEORGE BAKER, P.C., M.P.

Manly MacDonald (1889–1971)
Land Girls Hoeing, c. 1919
Oil on canvas
152.8 × 194.0 cm · CWM 8390

Eric Brown, director of the National Gallery, invited Manly MacDonald to paint near Belleville, Ontario, for the Canadian War Memorials Fund. He even suggested the subject matter. "I think there should be some fine landscape subjects in connection with girls' work on the land, farming of various kinds, fruit picking etc.; the clothes are picturesque and this side of the war work should certainly be pictured."

CONTENTS

FOREWORD

BECAUSE I WAS BORN in 1939, I had the demographic good luck to grow up in a rich, peaceful Canada. I was too young, of course, to be affected by the Second World War, and too young for the Korean War. Although I was in the army for ten years after 1956, I never heard a shot fired in anger. And because I went to university in an age of expansion, there were scholarships and opportunities aplenty. I married young, found a job and bought my first (and only) house when prices were low. For me and many Canadians like me, this was good luck, nothing more, a matter of being born in the right place at the right time.

Had I been born twenty years earlier, my life would have been very different. I would have reached my teens in the midst of the Depression, exactly the right age to go into the service when the Second World War broke out in 1939. University and marriage would have been put on hold. And I might very possibly have been killed or grievously wounded at Hong Kong or Dieppe, in the battles in Sicily, Italy, Normandy, the Scheldt, or in the 1945 campaign that liberated the Netherlands. If I'd joined the navy, I might have been drowned when HMCS *St Croix* was torpedoed on the North Atlantic; if I had enlisted in the air force, the odds were high that I might have been shot down in a Lancaster bomber over Germany's Ruhr valley. The good luck that let me thrive was not present for many of those born a mere

twenty years earlier than me. Forty-two thousand of the 1.1 million Canadian men and women who enlisted were killed or died in training during the Second World War.

If I had been born forty years earlier than I was, the First World War would have shaped my life. My chances of survival, in fact, would have been even less. One in ten of the 620,000 Canadians who enlisted in the Great War—the war to end wars—was killed.

My point is that war affected huge numbers of Canadians and changed or ended thousands of lives. Each of those killed in action left parents, siblings, spouses, children or friends. Each of those wounded required care, often for years. Lives were disrupted. So was the nation. One of those soldiers killed on the Somme might have written the great Canadian novel; one killed at Ortona might have discovered the cure for cancer.

Moreover, the good life that I enjoy has been shaped by the actions of those who fought for Canada. If the democracies had lost the Second World War, Canada would have been a very different place. Canadians today, sadly shortchanged by our school systems and left almost totally bereft of any historical understanding, scarcely realize to what they owe their good fortune. The veterans, now old men and women wearing their Legion blazers, berets and medals on November 11, were once the warriors who saved the world. The war workers who supplied our forces are long into retirement.

And the wars transformed Canada. The federal government grew exponentially, its controls and rationing affecting everyone. Linguistic tensions increased, while farmers worried over the loss of their sons to the army

William Beatty (1868–1941)
Ablain St-Nazaire, 1918
Oil on canvas
182.7 × 214.6 cm · CWM 8102

Originally a Toronto house and sign painter, and a fireman by trade, William Beatty had served as a soldier in the Northwest Campaign of 1885 before training in Europe as an artist. "The story of my life is not fit for publication," he once commented.

The Europe he discovered as a war artist was one of destruction, as his painting of Ablain-St. Nazaire near Vimy Ridge depicts. Beatty was one of the first four Canadian official war artists appointed by the Canadian War Memorials Fund (CWMF). He, Fred Varley, Maurice Cullen and Charles Simpson were given the rank of captain, and full military pay and allowances amounting to twenty-seven hundred dollars annually.

This was a considerable step down from his by then regular income as a teacher and artist. In a letter to Sir Edmund Walker, chairman of the Advisory Arts Council, the Canadian arm of the CWMF, Beatty commented that "the experience has cost me rather dearly up to the present time." His ongoing concerns regarding reimbursement for materials and other expenses in connection with his war work, concerns shared by other Canadian painters, underline the novelty of appointing full-time war artists in Canada. His resignation was accepted on August 1, 1919, but the requests for money went on until June 1920.

Gerald Moira (1867–1959)

Canadian Foresters in
Windsor Park, c. 1918

Oil on canvas
266.7 × 306.0 cm · CWM 8558

Many artists wanted to be war artists.
London-born Gerald Moira was no
different. "I should certainly like to go to
France . . . I should like to know the conditions under which artists are sent to the
Front. I would like the opportunity to do
Decorative paintings of the war for the
nation, & when one considers that the
Dominions have already sent out artists
to do Decorative paintings more or less
illustrative of the deeds of the
Contingents provided by them it is high
time the Mother Country should do the
same. . . . Now is the time to collect
impressions & details. . . . It is positively
essential that the country should have
memorials of the war & these should be
of a decorative character, so as once
[and] for all to do away with the Battle
pictures, painted at home."

and their daughters to the booming munitions factories in the city. In the Second World War, social policies finally began to be put in place, and the veterans' benefits improved markedly over those offered the old sweats from the Great War. Canada was vastly different in 1919 than it had been in 1914, and it was even more so in 1945 than in 1939.

This book, with its superb reproductions of Canada's war art and its fine text by Dean F. Oliver and Laura Brandon, inevitably stirs up these thoughts. The early paintings of the Great War resembled nothing so much as the heroic art of Wellington's victory at the Battle of Waterloo, or countless British colonial wars; the later works showed the destruction and horror of the trenches, the grievously wounded, the dead. They also illustrated the changing technology of war: from rifles to huge artillery pieces, from cavalry to tanks, from the ground-level view from the trenches to the savage beauty of air warfare, from wives and sweethearts at the railway station waving goodbye to their men to women making shells or working in the fields. The war art showed, through the acute eye of the artist, how war had changed and the ways in which war altered Canada. That the conflict also changed the way artists painted, that it largely created the style with which the Group of Seven, for instance, viewed the Canadian landscape, should also become immediately apparent to all who read this book.

The naiveté of Canadians in 1914 had disappeared from the population by 1939, and it similarly had evaporated for the nation's artists. Some seemed to revel in the technology—Lawren P. Harris's tanks roaring through dust and smoke in Italy, for example—but others, including Alex Colville and Aba Bayefsky, were traumatized by the horror. Colville and Bayefsky sketched the dead and the barely living at the Nazi concentration camp at Bergen-Belsen. Colville's wonderful painting of Canadian infantry plodding slowly along a Dutch polder similarly expressed a terrible weariness of spirit, a weariness that Fred Varley or A.Y. Jackson would have immediately understood during the Great War.

The superb paintings in this volume are only a small part of the wondrous collection of nearly 13,000 pieces of art held by the Canadian War Museum. This collection, likely the largest and least-known holding of Canadian war art anywhere, is a national treasure. This book, and the large exhibition touring Canada, will let Canadians see and appreciate some of the wonderful art that emerged from the horror of war. To read the text is simultaneously to learn more about the country's war history. As a former director of the Museum, as a historian, as a Canadian, I believe we all need to know more about how Canada reached its present place in the world.

J. L. GRANATSTEIN

After serving in the Canadian Army from 1956 to 1966, J. L. Granatstein taught Canadian history at York University for thirty years and published extensively in military, diplomatic and political history. From 1998 to 2000, he was the Director and Chief Executive Officer of the Canadian War Museum.

THE

FIRST

WORLD

WAR

BORN IN BATTLE

We must not forget that days may come when our patience, our endurance and our fortitude will be tried to the utmost. In those days let us see to it that no heart grows faint and that no courage be found wanting.
PRIME MINISTER SIR ROBERT BORDEN,
AUGUST 19, 1918, HOUSE OF COMMONS *DEBATES*

PRIME MINISTER Sir Robert Borden, like thousands of other Canadians, was enjoying a summer vacation in late July 1914. He had hoped to spend four weeks with his wife at Port Carling on Lake Muskoka, playing golf, swimming and recovering from carbuncles. Between holes on the back nine, the Conservative leader contemplated an early election call to spur reform of the Liberal-dominated Senate. It was not an easy time for his government. Amid high unemployment, drought and widespread dissatisfaction with his three-year administration, the news of impending war in Europe brought further trouble to his domain. Possibly it might rescue his party's fortunes by forcing Canadians to rally around their government, but in the short term its impact was clear: there would be little more golfing for Canada's prime minister in the summer of 1914.

At 8:55 P.M. on August 4, Borden received "the momentous telegram" announcing Britain's declaration of war. Immediately Canada and the rest of the Empire joined the cause, all for one and one for all, there

being no independent political tradition or legal precedent on which to base a separate Canadian resort to arms. Few would have wanted it in any case. When the Empire was at war, so too was Canada. English Canadians, including thousands of recent immigrants from the British Isles, flocked to the colours. For most Canadians, weaned on tales of military glory and imperial victories, duty demanded an immediate and enthusiastic reply to the call to arms. Even Borden's heartfelt response to Britain's predicament was muted compared with that of his Minister of Militia and Defence, Sam Hughes. For this volatile, bombastic veteran of the South African War, martial enthusiasm was a necessary precursor to national maturity. Having long predicted a day of reckoning with the Kaiser's Germany, Hughes now revelled in the challenge. The suggestion, by historian Sandra Gwyn, that Hughes was "almost certainly mad"[1] is resisted vigorously by Hughes's biographer, Ronald G. Haycock, for whom the minister was "formidable," "complicated," "individualistic" and "idiosyncratic," but sane.[2]

Hughes also reflected public attitudes. From the pulpits, priests and ministers spoke of Canada being purged and purified by war. Khaki had become a sacred colour, noted Samuel D. Chown, general superintendent of the Methodist Church. "A war in defence of weakness against strength, a war for truth and plighted pledge, for freedom against oppression, is God's war wherever waged," noted the *Presbyterian Record* in

Harrington Mann (1864–1937)
Sir Robert Borden, 1918
Oil on canvas
127.5 × 102.2 cm · CWM 8413

When commissioned to portray
Canada's wartime prime minister in 1918,
Harrington Mann, who was born in
Scotland and trained in Paris, was a
noted British portrait painter.

CANVAS OF WAR

Fred Varley (1881–1969)
For What?, c. 1918
Oil on canvas
147.2 × 182.8 cm · CWM 8911

In a letter dating from mid-May 1919 to his wife, Maud, this eminent Canadian artist summed up his feelings about the war. "I'm mighty thankful I've left France—I never want to see it again. This last trip over has put the tin hat on it. To see the land half cultivated & people coming back to where their homes were is too much for my make up. You'll never know dear anything of what it means. I'm going to paint a picture of it, but heavens, it can't say a thousandth part of a story. We'd be healthier to forget, & that we never can. We are for ever tainted with its abortiveness & its cruel drama—and for the life of me I don't know how that can help progression. It is foul and smelly—and heartbreaking. Sometimes I could weep my eyes out when I get despondent. . . . To be normal, to be as those silly cows & sheep that do naught but graze & die, well, it's forgetfulness."

Harrington Mann (1864–1937)
*Lieutenant General
Sir Sam Hughes*, 1918
Oil on canvas
127.3 × 102.2 cm · CWM 8414

This portrait reveals the pugnacious temperament that characterized Sir Sam Hughes's erratic leadership. The general was minister of militia during the first twenty-seven months of the First World War.

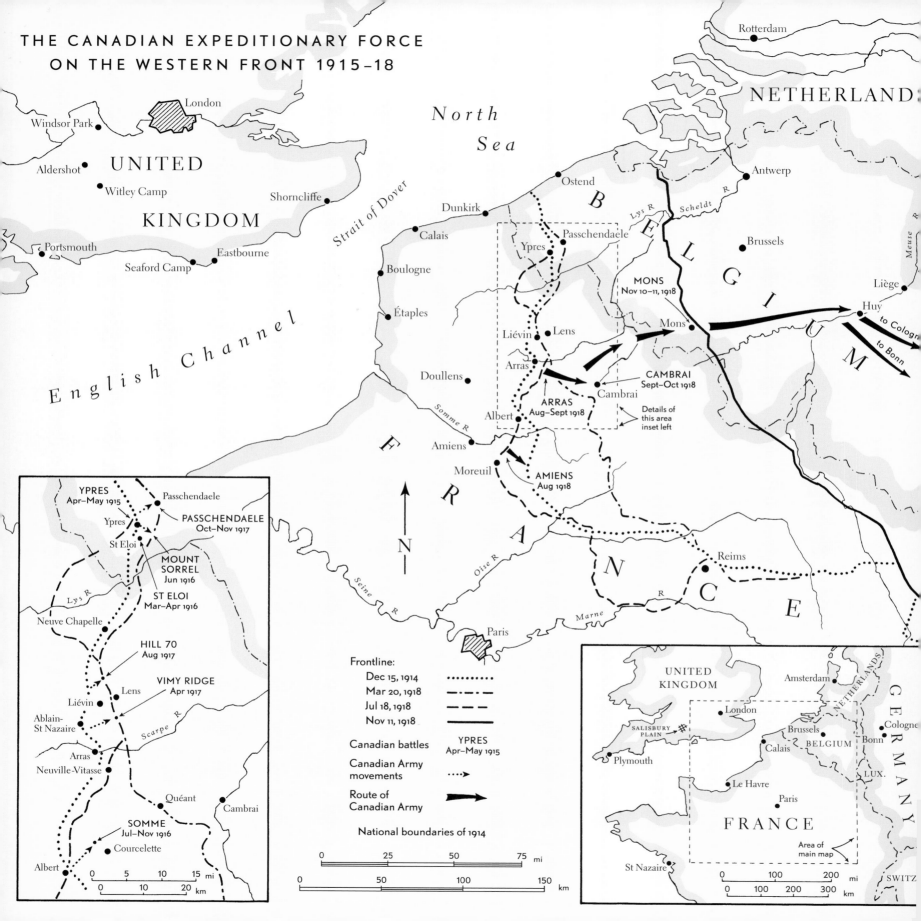

THE CANADIAN EXPEDITIONARY FORCE ON THE WESTERN FRONT 1915–18

NETHERLAND

North Sea

English Channel

Strait of Dover

UNITED KINGDOM

London
Windsor Park
Aldershot
Witley Camp
Shorncliffe
Portsmouth
Seaford Camp
Eastbourne

Rotterdam
Antwerp
Ostend
Dunkirk
Calais
Boulogne
Étaples
Brussels

B E L G I U M

Ypres
Passchendaele
Lys R
Scheldt R
Meuse R
Liège
Huy
to Cologne
to Bonn

MONS
Nov 10–11, 1918
Mons

Liévin
Lens
Arras
Cambrai

CAMBRAI
Sept–Oct 1918

Doullens

ARRAS
Aug–Sept 1918

Albert
Somme R

Details of this area inset left

Amiens
Moreuil

AMIENS
Aug 1918

F R A N C E

N

Seine R
Oise R
Marne R

Reims

Paris

Inset (lower left)

YPRES
Apr–May 1915
Ypres
Passchendaele

PASSCHENDAELE
Oct–Nov 1917

St Eloi

MOUNT SORREL
Jun 1916

ST ELOI
Mar–Apr 1916

Neuve Chapelle
Lys R

HILL 70
Aug 1917

VIMY RIDGE
Apr 1917

Liévin
Lens

Ablain-St Nazaire
Scarpe R

Arras
Neuville-Vitasse
Quéant
Cambrai

SOMME
Jul–Nov 1916
Courcelette
Albert

0 5 10 15 mi
0 10 20 km

Legend

Frontline:
Dec 15, 1914 ....
Mar 20, 1918 –·–·–·–
Jul 18, 1918 – – – –
Nov 11, 1918 ———

Canadian battles   YPRES
                    Apr–May 1915

Canadian Army movements ·····▶

Route of Canadian Army ███▶

National boundaries of 1914

0   25   50   75 mi
0   50   100   150 km

Inset (lower right)

UNITED KINGDOM

SALISBURY PLAIN

London
Plymouth

Amsterdam
NETHERLANDS

Brussels
BELGIUM
Calais
LUX.
Cologne
Bonn

GERMANY

Le Havre

Paris

FRANCE

St Nazaire

SWITZ.

Area of main map

0   100   200 mi
0   100   200   300 km

October 1914.[3] Rifle association presidents and grey-haired militia organizers delighted in the rarefied atmosphere of patriotism and imperial pride. Canadian public opinion exuded confidence in an early victory over the Germans. Most major European wars in the nineteenth century had ended quickly, so why not this one? Moreover, how could good not triumph over evil?

In Canada as in France, Britain or Australia, politicians, generals and the men and women they would lead spoke rashly about "getting in" before it was all over. Recruits wanted to "have a go" before the war ended. The atmosphere was electric, surreal. Crowds from Halifax to Victoria cheered the war's outbreak. "Montreal teemed with suppressed anxiety," wrote Louis Keene, a soldier and artist. On the evening of August 4, "one met demonstrations everywhere, large crowds of cheering men with flags, Victrolas at shop windows played patriotic airs, and civilians crowded before the bulletin boards singing the national anthems with great enthusiasm."[4] Overnight, soldiering became a noble profession. Canadians would make war to ensure peace, noted an editorial in the Toronto *Globe* on September 28, and they would be united in the struggle. At first it was true. The early battles, and early defeats, for Britain, France and Russia were devastating blows, but the German steamroller was at last turned aside just east of Paris, and aspects of the war's early months passed quickly into legend. Heroic Belgium resisting the advancing German hordes, the epic retreat of British forces and their valiant stand at Ypres, France's taxi

cab army which saved Paris at the Battle of the Marne: these and other stirring tales combined to stiffen Allied resolve. They were also terrific material for recruiting campaigns. At Mons, according to some accounts, even the angels had come to Britain's aid.

Across Canada, civilian organizations and charitable societies turned their considerable energies to assisting the war effort. The spirit of volunteerism and sacrifice flourished. Conservative and Liberal politicians joined forces to support an unprecedented level of government involvement in Canadians' economic, political and social affairs. The resulting War Measures Act (1914) authorized sweeping emergency powers for the federal government in the event of "war, invasion or insurrection, real or apprehended." In 1915, taking the unusual step of collecting money for the war from ordinary Canadians, Ottawa asked for $50 million in voluntary contributions and raised twice that amount.

Patriotic newspapers kept domestic readers up to date, more or less, with events at the front. In Canada, as in all the Allied nations, recriminations over bad generalship and poor equipment, ammunition shortages, and disputes over command and jurisdiction marred the war effort from the start, but press censorship helped ensure at least that public morale would not sag through creeping defeatism. Generals would spend years searching for the winning military combination, in the process expending hundreds of thousands of lives, tens of thousands of them young Canadians, but public attitudes grew only modestly more reluctant as the war dragged on and casualties increased. In Canada, old men and self-appointed recruiting officers would continue to extol the virtues of service-in-arms while earnest ladies mocked the cowardice of able-bodied males who remained at home. But as one ferocious battle followed another, it became more and more difficult to entice young men away from their homes and families. Although Prime Minister Borden promised at the outset that Canadians would not be conscripted, it was unclear what might happen if the supply of volunteers dried up. In the heady summer and fall of 1914, it seemed a distant worry.

OFF TO WAR

Canada's enthusiastic First Contingent of men for service in Europe, thirty-three thousand strong, assembled at a huge makeshift camp at Valcartier, twenty-six kilometres northwest of Quebec City, soon after the declaration of war. They should not have been there at all. Sam Hughes scrapped the carefully laid regional mobilization plans of his senior military officer to issue instead a direct call for volunteers. The response was huge and thousands of men arrived from all across the country. The spectacle was grand, but chaotic. Some support units, including artillery and medical formations, assembled elsewhere under the old mobilization scheme before proceeding to Valcartier, but at the five-thousand-hectare camp carved out quickly from the Quebec wilderness, Hughes himself organized the various incoming troops.

Following standard military practice for the day, the basic building block of Canada's war effort would be the infantry battalion. Four such battalions, each of roughly one thousand men, formed a brigade, and three brigades (or twelve battalions), plus artillery, medical, engineering and other support units, formed the 1st Canadian Division. Brigades, for the most part, contained battalions recruited from the same part of the country. All recruits received rudimentary military training and fired a few practice rounds from hastily acquired Ross rifles, but there was little time (or expertise) for much more preparation than that. After several weeks of frantic effort, in early October, the First Contingent, which included all the troops needed for the 1st Division and large additional numbers to replace casualties, piled onto ships and sailed down the St. Lawrence River for England.

T. V. Anderson, a military engineer and future chief of the general staff, remembered the voyage as largely uneventful, noting that the troops handled "all the discomforts . . . remarkably well," but he was not in the majority. E. L. Christopherson of the 5th Battalion recalled that his ship, the *Lapland*, was crawling with lice. In a few hours, "we were just as lousy as pet coons [raccoons], the whole bunch of us." R. S. Timmis was with a cavalry unit, the Royal Canadian Dragoons, whose horses were infected by ringworm during the long voyage in cramped, dirty ships. An officer in the Fort Garry Horse, another mounted unit, after inquiring whether his men had complaints about the food,

James Quinn (1871–1951)
Major O. M. Learmonth,
the Victoria Cross, 1918
Oil on canvas
101.6 × 76.5 cm · CWM 8682

Australian-born and Paris-trained,
James Quinn undertook portrait commissions for both the Australians and the
Canadians. Major Learmonth, born in
Quebec City, was a twenty-three-year-old
officer in the 2nd Battalion, Canadian
Expeditionary Force, when he died from
wounds received during the successful
Canadian assault on Hill 70 on August
18, 1917. In the words of the citation:
"For most conspicuous bravery and
exceptional devotion to duty. During
a determined counter-attack on our new
positions, this officer, when his company
was momentarily surprised, instantly
charged and personally disposed of
the attackers. Later, he carried on a
tremendous fight with the advancing
enemy. Although under intense barrage
fire and mortally wounded he stood on
the parapet of the trench, bombed the
enemy continuously and directed the
defence in such a manner as to infuse a
spirit of utmost resistance into his men.
On several occasions this very brave
officer actually caught bombs thrown
at him by the enemy and threw them
back. When he was unable by reason of
his wounds to carry on the fight he still
refused to be carried out of the line,
and continued to give instructions and
invaluable advice to his junior officers,
finally handing over all duties before
he was evacuated from the front line to
the hospital where he died."

9

facing page:

Algernon Talmage (1871–1939)
The Sulphur Dip for Mange, c. 1918
Oil on canvas
51.0 × 61.3 cm · CWM 8833

Veterinary units and over seven thousand horses sailed with Canada's First Contingent to England in October 1914. At its greatest strength, the Canadian Corps had more than 23,500 horses. Most of English artist Algernon Talmage's paintings were based on time spent near Quéant, on the Hindenburg Line, in 1918.

left:

Charles Sims (1873–1928)
Sacrifice, c. 1918
Oil on canvas
415.2 × 409.0 cm · CWM 8802

The most religious of the large Canadian War Memorials paintings, *Sacrifice* is also the most nationalistic. In the original oil study, the English artist had the figure of Christ facing the viewer. In the plans for Lord Beaverbrook's never-built war memorial art gallery in Ottawa, this painting takes pride of place. "The apotheosis by Charles Sims will be declaimed from the halls around the Central Dome," wrote Paul Konody, Beaverbrook's artistic adviser on the Canadian War Memorials Fund committee, in *Art and War* in 1919.

was struck in the face twice by rotten kippers tossed anonymously by his unappreciative men.[5] "It is really remarkable," wrote Louis Keene, "how they can consistently get that same coal-oil flavor in all the food."[6]

The troops' arrival was boisterous, rude and memorable. "Large crowds lined the streets and the road to the [train] station, giving us cigarettes, matches, apples and papers," Private Victor Swanston, 5th Battalion, recorded in his diary on October 20. "Kisses were freely exchanged all the way. I wrote my address on an Army 'Hard-tack' [biscuit] and gave it to the best looking girl I saw."[7] Many soldiers went absent without leave, drinking to excess and carousing with the locals. "There followed a week of dizzy, lurid days," recalled Arthur Hunt Chute, an officer from Nova Scotia. "[Rudyard] Kipling said that we painted Plymouth pink, but that is putting it mild. We painted Plymouth red."[8] After their long sea voyage and several frustrating days lying at anchor off Plymouth, most Canadians were simply thankful to be off the ship and on dry land. With some difficulty, British troops and Canadian officers gathered up and sent the multitude to Salisbury Plain for more training.

It rained for 89 of the next 123 days, making the Canadians' first encampments cold, wet and miserable. "Early in December," recalled John Sutton, a British-born gunner, "the rain became almost continuous, sometimes quite heavy. The summer tents with no floor boards were almost as wet inside as outside. . . . The dirt roads had become almost impassable. Drill grounds and horse lines were almost quagmires." In these

conditions, twenty-eight men died from meningitis. There were other problems as well. Much of the equipment carried by the troops, especially that provided by eager Canadian contractors, proved useless, while the Canadians' basic training required extensive polishing. Although the division had arrived in England in rapid time, much to the surprise of some professional officers, the men were still not a fighting force. British Lieutenant-General Sir E. A. H. Alderson, the division commander, worked hard in the fall of 1914 to ready his men for battle.

Moving into France in February 1915, three months after one battalion, Princess Patricia's Canadian Light Infantry, part of the British 27th Division, had already arrived, the division prepared for action by serving a week at the front under the close eye of British units. This instruction was absolutely necessary but also a mixed blessing. Britain's veteran troops were certainly better placed to tell the fresh Canadians a thing or two about their German enemies, but were themselves still learning the basics of trench warfare. British defensive practice, for example, crammed troops into trenches near the front lines that made the soldiers rich targets for German artillery and machine guns, leading to high casualties in the early stages of an attack and leaving little reserve strength to counterattack if the Germans broke through the defensive line. Only later would the British and Canadians learn to defend lightly up front and hold larger forces in the rear.

Norman Wilkinson (1878–1971)
Canada's Answer, c. 1918
Oil on canvas
214.6 × 367.6 cm · CWM 8934

Canada's First Contingent of over thirty-three thousand partially trained troops sailed to Britain in thirty transport ships in October 1914. Here, the big Royal Navy battlecruiser HMS *Princess Royal* leads the convoy as it nears Britain's coast. A British marine painter, Norman Wilkinson achieved fame for inventing the dazzle-painting technique, a form of camouflage applied to a ship's hull to make it more difficult to detect. In his April 1917 proposal to the British War Office, he described it as "large patches of strong colour in a carefully thought out pattern and colour scheme."

14   CANVAS OF WAR

facing page:

Thurstan Topham (1888–1966)
The Artist's Own Dug-Out on the
Albert-Braye Roadside, 1916
Watercolour on paper
21.9 × 28.2 cm · CWM 8896

According to his military records, Thurstan Topham's assignment with the 1st Canadian Siege Battery to make panoramic observation sketches for military intelligence and gun-ranging purposes was cut short by an early exposure to gas. Two months in France at the height of the Battle of the Somme resulted in two years in a variety of hospitals and medical facilities before he was discharged. The collection of fifty sketches by the then little-known artist, for which he was paid five hundred dollars by the Canadian War Memorials in 1919, includes this one of his own dugout. As he later wrote, his often moonlit renditions of the front were "'unofficial' personal sketches done under considerable handicap."

left:

Harold Mowat (1879–1949)
Trench Fight, c. 1918
Conté and wash on cardboard
50.8 × 38.0 cm · CWM 8562

The Canadian War Records Office in London, England, hired artilleryman Harold Mowat as an artist shortly after he arrived in England in July 1917. In a series of black-and-white drawings, he captured the grim reality of service on the western front.

15

In early March, Alderson's troops entered the trenches for the first time as a complete division. It was not a comfortable or comforting experience. "The trenches in many cases had water up to your knees," recalled T. V. Anderson. "Some of them were almost impassible."[9] Sandbags were so scarce that, on occasion, Canadians raided the German trenches to steal theirs. A week later the Canadians provided covering fire for an attack by British troops against German positions around Neuve Chapelle. After more than twelve thousand casualties, including one hundred or so Canadians, the attack failed despite some initial successes. As would happen all too frequently on the western front, where German troops confronted British, French and Belgian forces from the Franco-Swiss border to the English Channel, the German defenders were able to seal off breaches in their lines far more quickly than British troops could exploit them. Trying to overcome this race against time with better tactics, technology and training would be a central feature of military planning on both sides for the rest of the war.

By the spring of 1915, the western front had settled into a long line of opposing trenches. Entire divisions of Allied cavalry waited behind the lines in vain to exploit a breakthrough while infantry, engineers and gunners faced off across all-but-unbreachable rows of barbed wire, artillery emplacements and machine-gun nests. It was not what most pre-war experts had predicted. Rain, snow and repeated artillery barrages would gradually turn the ground between the German and Franco-British lines into an almost impenetrable morass of mud and shell holes. Even natural features such as small hills and ridges would later be swept away by years of shelling, leaving an almost featureless moonscape in its wake. But in 1915, it was still possible for Alderson's troops to recognize towns, landmarks and topography.

April 1915 found the Canadian division defending a section of the front near Ypres, Belgium, where, in October–November 1914, retreating British forces had fought a gallant rearguard action against the advancing Germans (the First Battle of Ypres). Many civilians had not yet fled the badly bombed town, and farmers went about their business just behind the Canadian lines. This semblance of normalcy did not last long. On April 22, the Germans attacked, using a new weapon for the first time on the western front. A light breeze carried clouds of chlorine gas towards the Allied lines, where it caught French and Algerian troops by surprise and sent them reeling, leaving the Canadians dangerously exposed with enemy troops closing in on them from three sides. Several days of vicious, confused fighting followed, during which the inexperienced, outnumbered Canadians, along with British battalions that rushed in to fill the gap, held the salient against repeated German attacks. The fighting claimed more than sixty-seven hundred Canadian casualties but established for the men of the division a reputation as tenacious and effective troops. Historian D. J. Goodspeed observed that the Second Battle of Ypres gave "the Canadians an *esprit de corps* they never lost."[10]

Anna Airy (1882–1964)

Cookhouse, Witley Camp, 1918
Oil on canvas
304.8 × 381.0 cm · CWM 8009

One museum noted the following information on Anna Airy, a well-known British artist, which may explain why she was one of the few woman painters employed during the war. "In the early years of the century she penetrated into Thames-side haunts of vice and crime in search of human nature in the raw. She has witnessed prize-fights without gloves, and cock-fights. She was present in an underground gambling den when murder was committed, and only escaped the police cordon by the wit of a card-sharper friend."

In 1984, Lee Murray, the Canadian War Museum's chief curator, quaintly described *Cookhouse, Witley Camp*: "Here is portrayed an amusing scene of army life in a Reserve camp. The painting is not without that touch of humour which is rarely absent from the artist's work, as may be noted by the action of the figure in the foreground. The interior is of a regional cook-house at Witley Camp, Surrey, in 1917. At the time the 156th Canadian Infantry Battalion was at the training camp."

facing page:

A.Y. Jackson (1882–1974)

Houses of Ypres, 1917

Oil on canvas

63.8 × 76.8 cm · CWM 8207

As he noted in his autobiography, A.Y. Jackson had clear ideas on the role of artists in wartime: "It is logical that artists should be a part of the organization of total war, whether to provide inspiration, information, or comment on the glory or the stupidity of war." He continued: "What to paint was a problem for the war artist. There was nothing to serve as a guide. War had gone underground, and there was little to see. The old heroics, the death and glory stuff, were gone for ever; there was no more 'Thin Red Line' or 'Scotland For Ever.' . . . The impressionist technique I had adopted in painting was now ineffective, for visual impressions were not enough."

left:

Private A.Y. Jackson at 258 Bishop St., Montreal, 1915. A.Y. Jackson wrote an account of his meeting with Lord Beaverbrook. "I awaited his arrival in his office where his little secretary, Sgt. Alexander, had his mail all arranged in piles of greater and lesser importance. He was poised with his notebook ready when His Lordship blew in like a cyclone. Beaverbrook read rapidly through the first letters, and began a running fire of instructions to Alexander. 'Tell Winston Churchill I will have lunch with him tomorrow at one. Tell Bonar Law I will see him at eight o'clock tonight. Tell Lloyd George to meet me on Thursday afternoon at four.' He looked at me; for a moment he had forgotten who I was. Then, 'Alexander,' he said, 'make this man a lieutenant.' "

Photo courtesy of Dr. Naomi Jackson Groves National Gallery of Canada 15.4.80

They still had much to learn. Propaganda at home and in England presented the colonial troops from Canada, Australia and elsewhere as natural warriors. Described as the rough-and-tumble woodcutters, farmers, miners, fishermen and pioneers of popular literature and magazines, most of the troops were from the cities, like their British, French and German counterparts. Of the quarter million men who had enlisted by March 1, 1916, 65 per cent had been manual labourers before the war; another 18.5 per cent had been clerks. Only 6.5 per cent had been farmers or ranchers. More frontiersmen and hearty farmers had enrolled by war's end, but in 1918, industrial workers still outnumbered farmers, fishermen and lumbermen by more than 60 per cent, and there were more white-collar workers than farmers. More than one-third of those who joined the Canadian Expeditionary Force (CEF), the administrative title for Canada's army overseas during the war, reported previous military experience, the vast majority of them in the pre-war militia, but 18,959 were former members of the British army. The Canadian troops were blessed with several good commanders and staff officers, including many British officers attached to the force at the start of the war, but there were many bad officers too. As with all armies surprised by the onset of trench warfare, the men of the CEF learned the soldiering trade in the school of hard knocks.

Plenty of little things helped to keep soldiers alive, such as building proper trenches and dugouts, ensuring adequate hygiene and maintaining personal kit and equipment in good order. There were bigger things too, such as properly coordinating artillery, infantry, aircraft and, later, tanks. Good intelligence and effective leadership were also keys to battlefield success and survival. Nothing could be taken for granted. At St. Eloi, Belgium, in 1916, Canadian commanders literally lost thousands of their men. Claiming to have captured their objectives, a series of vast craters created by huge underground explosions, all of which looked alike in the devastated, muddy earth, the Canadians, in fact, had seized different objectives entirely. Their understandable error resulted in a nasty defeat for the poorly prepared, badly positioned Canadians. "We were walking on dead soldiers," wrote Sergeant Frank Maheux, a former logger from the Ottawa Valley, to his wife, "and the worse was they was [sic] about 3 feet of mud and water. I saw poor fellows trying to bandage their wounds, bombs, heavy shells falling all over them . . . it is the worst sight that a man ever wants to see."[11] In battles at Mount Sorrel and along the Somme in 1916, the Canadians learned that careful planning, teamwork and high morale could overcome some, but not all, of the difficulties of trench warfare. From September to November, during the last phase of the costly British offensive along the Somme, the Canadians attacked repeatedly German positions near the small town of Courcelette. Twenty-four thousand soldiers were killed and wounded for an advance of just six kilometres.

Time in the trenches was long, excruciating and tense. It grated on the nerves, sometimes breaking even

Edgar Bundy (1862–1922)

Landing of the First Canadian Division at Saint-Nazaire, c. 1918

Oil on canvas

259.0 × 457.0 cm · CWM 8121

An English artist, Edgar Bundy was commissioned to commemorate the landing of the 3rd Canadian Infantry Brigade at St. Nazaire, France, in February 1915. The band of the Black Watch marches in the left foreground while to the right stand Canadian Generals Richard Turner and Frederick Loomis, and the minister of militia, Sir Sam Hughes. The steamship *Novian* dominates the background of this large painting that now hangs in the Senate Chamber in Ottawa.

Louis Weirter (1873–1932)
The Battle for Courcelette, 1918
Oil on canvas
304.8 × 609.7 cm · CWM 8931

The capture of Courcelette on
September 15, 1916, is considered one of
the Canadians' greatest achievements
during the Battle of the Somme. In a
departure from many of the battle-scene
commissions of others, Scottish-born
Louis Weirter actually witnessed the
events he depicted. A serving soldier
throughout the war and a major contrib-
utor to the discipline of field sketching,
the painter also invented the Weirter
rangefinder for use by aircraft. He attrib-
uted his technological innovations to a
love of perspective.

William Nicholson (1872–1949)

Canadian Headquarters Staff, 1918

Oil on canvas

242.0 × 292.1 cm · CWM 8671

A group portrait of Generals Richard Turner, Alexander McRae, Harold McDonald, Gilbert Foster and Percival Thacker and Major Furry Montague. In style and mood, the composition owes much to the portraits of Malcolm Arbuthnot, who had photographed William Nicholson's children in uniform a year earlier, in poses similar to those of the generals. The English artist found the commission trying. To his son Ben he wrote on April 7, 1918: "My Canadians make slow progress, it's a Hell of a job."

the hardest of men. Listening to Canadian guns bombarding the German lines on New Year's Eve, 1916, Winnipeg's Herbert Burrell questioned the absurdity of it all. "Who in the world, this time last year would have dreamt that on its anniversary I would be lying in a dugout in France writing up my diary while cannon, bombs and machine guns make hideous the vanishing hours of 1916." Private Tom Dinesen, who would later win the Victoria Cross, the Empire's highest award for gallantry in battle, remembered ten men living in a tiny dugout at the front: "The dirt and the vermin, the thick, full-flavoured air—all this only serves to increase our feelings of comfort when we sit together here, warm and safe, chatting, singing and burning our fingers vainly endeavouring to make a basin of porridge boil over a sardine tin filled with bacon grease and with a wick made of rags from a piece of sandbag."[12]

Life along the front was not all battles, nor was all a soldier's time spent there. Units rotated to and from the front lines on a regular basis, and even when posted in the line of battle, not all men were on the edge of no man's land at the same time. Each unit kept a reserve and alternated its men accordingly. Troops several hundred yards behind the front were still at risk from artillery, air attacks and, more ominously, disease, but they enjoyed better accommodations, more normal sleep patterns and, generally, more enticing food. Farther to the rear, in designated rest areas or in civilian billets in towns, the troops relaxed and enjoyed such comforts as wartime Europe could

offer, including, of course, alcohol and sex. As Robert Swan, an infantry officer, suggested in verse:

On a dirty night when your nerves draw tight
And you rouse to the gas alarms,
In a dank shell hole you'd sell your soul
For a night in a woman's arms.[13]

Canadian overseas medical authorities in both world wars fought a running battle against sexually transmitted diseases, encouraging safe sex and regular medical examinations, at a time when even providing helpful sexual advice was controversial. Because Canada's social norms in the early twentieth century were extremely conservative, the knowledge that Canada's sons, husbands and brothers might have been overindulging their appetites in Europe would not have been popular with families at home. And although prohibition of alcohol was also common in Canada at the time, with advocates arguing that national purity was necessary to keep faith with those suffering at the front, most soldiers, when out of the line for a brief rest period, were distinctly less reluctant to indulge.

Away from the front lines, Canadian units trained in anticipation of their return to battle. Some instruction was routine—marksmanship or security precautions, for example—but there was also a concerted effort to ensure that the lessons of recent fighting found their way into Canadian battle methods before the next big push. Although for decades most writers on the First World War criticized its generals for stupidity and clumsiness,

Kenneth Forbes (1892–1980)
Canadian Artillery in Action, c. 1918
Oil on canvas
157.5 × 245.3 cm · CWM 8158

For Kenneth Forbes, then in the British Army, the call to become a war artist in 1918 was unexpected, but perhaps not unwelcome. He had been wounded twice and gassed. "I had been in the front line trenches for over two years and had just been promoted to second-in-command of the 32nd Machine Gun Co. which includes the rank of Captain, when I received an order to report to Col. Barry . . . he informed me that I was to report to the Canadian War Memorials, London and be transferred to the Canadian Army."

Canadian Artillery in Action reconstructs an incident on July 16, 1916, during the Battle of the Somme. Suffering under an intense barrage that resulted in many casualties, the Canadian gunners nevertheless stayed at their posts.

Eric Kennington (1888–1960)

The Conquerors, 1920
Oil on canvas
297.8 × 242.8 cm · CWM 8968

The dead and the living walk together through the shattered, symbol-littered landscape of the western front in this painting, which was originally entitled *The Victims.* As in a late medieval altarpiece, below their feet rests a skeleton, a form of memento mori. Some of the living are clearly dying, their legs metamorphosing into the quagmire through which they march.

A future governor general of Canada, Lord Tweedsmuir, had a poor opinion of the British artist's work. "I am very doubtful about Eric Kennington," he wrote, "his whole style of work is utterly remote from and undescriptive of the western front, and is no use for purposes of record. He might just as well paint his pictures at home."

Kennington's own assessment of his war art is interesting, and perhaps ironic given the powerful imagery in *The Conquerors.* "[I] did not attempt to depict any of the horror & tragedy, realizing that it was too vast & that I was not capable. . . ."

Nevertheless, he enjoyed being a war artist. "Had a warm reception everywhere artists are welcomed at front. The difficulty is that if an artist remains back he is safe & comfortable & does not really see the war, & if he goes really 'forward' he sees the war, and life is so disturbed and full of apprehensions, dangers and sudden changes that he cannot really apply himself to his work."

Sir William Orpen (1878–1931)

Lieutenant General Arthur Currie, 1919

Oil on canvas

91.8 × 71.5 cm · CWM 8673

The leading portrait painter of his age, Sir William Orpen, an Irishman, painted a number of Canadian generals. A majority of the works retain an unfinished appearance because, as he wrote: "They were really done as studies for a big portrait group of General Currie and other Canadian heroes."

Currie sat for his portrait in his rooms at the Ritz Hotel in Paris during the opening of the Peace Conference early in 1919. He never liked the result and, in 1924, requested that the painting be removed from an exhibition at the National Gallery of Canada. "I have never met anyone but who disliked the present portrait, except, of course, my enemies, who may regard it as satisfactory. I cannot imagine that at any time I looked as Orpen has portrayed me, and I think it unfair to future citizens of Canada, to Canada's war effort and to myself, to have that portrait handed down to posterity as a likeness of the Canadian Corps Commander." Sir Edmund Walker, chairman of the gallery's board of trustees, obliged.

Canadian generals, and a great many other generals as well, proved extremely eager to learn from their mistakes. They were not butchers, although many were overwhelmed by the nature of modern warfare and therefore sometimes appeared profligate with the lives of those they commanded. Herbert Burrell, who like most soldiers knew little of his commanders' efforts to learn from their mistakes, nevertheless condemned with a broad brush: "They play a baby warfare compared to the men, and with a few exceptions are a useless bunch."

For good officers, learning took many forms, including establishing specialist training schools and courses, widely circulating documents with titles such as "Notes on Recent Fighting" and constantly changing the training and organization of combat formations to apply the war's lessons. Tragically, it also included losing the lives of hundreds of thousands of soldiers as generals struggled to overcome the riddle of the trenches. Which army or national contingent adapted most quickly to such changes is still a subject of great controversy, although most historians agree that the Germans were probably the first. On the Allied side, many historians concede that the Canadians were the best of the bunch. Under both Lieutenant-General Sir Julian Byng, the outstanding British officer who commanded the corps in 1916–17, and Lieutenant-General Sir Arthur Currie, the brilliant Canadian militia officer who succeeded Byng, meticulous planning and carefully prepared attacks, the "set piece" battle, marked the Canadian style of war.

The Battle of Vimy Ridge in April 1917 proved that Canadian methods had improved immensely since 1915. Attacking German positions that had withstood several previous Allied assaults, the Canadian Corps, by now consisting of four divisions of infantry plus thousands of supporting troops (nearly one hundred thousand men in all), scored a quick and impressive victory by capturing almost the entire ridge, some six kilometres long and up to four kilometres wide, in a single day. "They were piling the gunfire ahead of us," recalled one soldier of the 25th Battalion, grateful for the supporting fire of friendly artillery, "plowing up everything ahead of you. A rat couldn't live on that ridge."[14] The success, hailed in Europe and at home as a brilliant military achievement, also marked an important phase in the evolution of the country. Historian Pierre Berton and many others have said that modern Canada, as a proud, independent, confident nation-state, was born on Vimy Ridge because there, for the first time in the war, all four of Canada's field divisions, including men from coast to coast, fought side by side to win the day. "I have always felt that Canadian nationality was born on the top of Vimy Ridge," remembered E. W. Russenholt, who was promoted to the rank of lieutenant in the 44th Battalion just before the battle. "There was a feeling that we had mastered this job and that we were the finest troops on earth. This is where Canadian nationality first came together when all of us were fused or welded, if you like, into a unity."[15] Even in victory, however, the battle exacted a high cost: 10,600 Canadian

above:

Cyril Barraud (1877–1965)

The Stretcher-Bearer Party, c. 1918
Oil on canvas
86.7 × 214.3 cm · CWM 8021

Winnipeg artist Cyril Barraud went
overseas with the 43rd Battalion of
the Canadian Expeditionary Force in
August 1915. In November 1917 he
was attached for duty to the Canadian
War Records Office (CWRO). He
sketched constantly on the front. The
CWRO sold these works, which were
transformed into etchings, for two
to five pounds each.

facing page:

Colin Gill (1892–1940)

Canadian Observation Post, 1920
Oil on canvas
185.5 × 243.0 cm · CWM 8967

The anguish of the shell-shock victim
to the right of the composition was a
grim reality for many veterans of the war.
English artist Colin Gill's correspon-

dence never speaks of this particular
despair, but more on the work to be
done. "I spent one night at Arras and
then came on up the line and have
been living at this battery position for
a week. . . . Weather is superb—but
freezing hard which with the short
hours of daylight makes work somewhat
difficult. Still, I am getting used now
to being cold and frost bitten! . . . I am
working in an improvised studio on
some sketches already begun."

casualties, including nearly 3600 dead. The Canadians were proving to be diligent students of the art of war, but every lesson came drenched in blood.

THE HOME FRONT WAR

Back at home, not everyone wanted to make the sacrifices that government propaganda and majority opinion claimed essential for the cause. The prime minister's 1914 pledge of fifty thousand troops for the war effort had, by January 1916, grown into a promise of five hundred thousand, or more than 6 per cent of Canada's entire pre-war population. The steadily growing casualty lists, especially the numbers of badly wounded and amputee soldiers now on Canadian streets, were not inducements to recruiting. Social, economic and labour problems also left many Canadians wondering whether or not the war would truly lead to a better Canada. Many wealthy business owners and speculators made their fortunes by selling to the government and to their fellow citizens while ordinary Canadians suffered from food and fuel shortages, inflation and unprecedented government interference in their lives. Doris Rosenburg, a Romanian immigrant living in Toronto, raised a family of ten during the war but had to fight inflation, scarcity and the black market every step of the way. "You managed," she later recalled, "you tried to do the best with what you had."[16]

There were probably not nearly as many war profiteers as disgruntled workers and enraged labour leaders believed or claimed, but there were more than enough to justify popular concerns. Moreover, the high cost of goods and services, aggravated by inflation caused by Ottawa's borrowing to pay its war expenses, led to hundreds of strikes by cash-strapped workers; new laws to tax business profits and personal income, to prevent potentially subversive assemblies and to make people work; and to the suppression of socialists, "radicals" and "enemy aliens" (immigrants from countries with which Canada was now at war). The rapid rise in union membership during the war led some people to worry that Bolshevik unrest would overturn the Canadian government just as it toppled the Russian Imperial family in 1917. The fact that most unionists merely wanted decent wages and working conditions did not prevent widespread surveillance, harassment and suppression by employers and the state.

Did motives count? Borden and many other opinion leaders believed strongly that Canada should do everything possible to support the war effort, but how far would the government go in order to do it? Declining numbers of volunteers for the military, coupled with the incessant complaints of English Canadians that French Canadians were not joining up in sufficient numbers, placed severe pressure on the government to implement conscription. After visiting the Vimy battlefield in May 1917, Borden himself concluded that failing to replace casualties at the front, by whatever means necessary, would constitute a tremendous disgrace for Canada, not least in the eyes of the troops. In France, the prime minister wrote soon afterwards, he had "the privilege of looking into the eyes of tens of thousands of men at the

Richard Jack (1866–1952)

The Taking of Vimy Ridge, Easter Monday 1917, 1919

Oil on canvas

366.1 × 604.5 cm · CWM 8178

Of Canada's many First World War battles, the successful assault at Vimy Ridge in April 1917 is the most famous. Victory cost more than ten thousand casualties. "Battle Vimy Ridge," Lieutenant H. L. Scott of the Canadian Engineers wrote in his diary, "Heavy return fire. The whole earth seemed to be in the air. When in air, came down to be blown up again. Worst battle in history of war to date. Hundreds blinded, arms and legs off. One man without any arms and legs still living."

Richard Jack's depiction avoids this tragic cost and concentrates instead on the technology that enabled the assault to succeed.

Gyrth Russell (1892–1970)
The Crest of Vimy Ridge, 1918
Oil on canvas
92.0 × 127.5 cm · CWM 8756

Vimy Ridge was a national symbol even before the war ended. Many Canadian artists found themselves sketching in its vicinity, resulting in a remarkable and varied visual document of the area as it looked in the last year of the war. Gyrth Russell was one of them.

He recalled his appointment as a war artist, an occasion on which he was clearly in awe of Lord Beaverbrook, the head of the Canadian War Memorials Fund and an erstwhile pupil of Russell's lawyer father. "Art critic [Paul] Konody, arranged an interview for me in the Minotaur's lair, somewhere in the labyrinth behind Fleet Street. I can't say we hit it off exactly, but he was eventually persuaded that my help was essential for a successful recording and I was enrolled as an Officer of the Canadian Army." Russell sketched in the field, afterwards producing watercolours, oils and a print series.

front who look to us for the effort which will make their sacrifice serve the great purpose for which it was undertaken."[17] Breaking faith with the struggling soldiers, who fully expected such relief, would also mean reducing Canada's overall contribution to the war by lowering the size and strength of its military forces overseas. Could Canada claim a rightful place among nations after the conflict if it had not done everything possible to secure the victory?

Such considerations were not shared by all Canadians, including many who believed that the war in Europe was not a Canadian concern, many who needed sons and husbands at home to harvest crops or others who held that the war benefited big business and the arms industry, the merchants of death. Because the conscription debate touched upon other important social issues, including disputes over language, culture, education, urban versus rural political priorities and class, Borden's determination to support the war at almost all costs set the stage for one of the nastiest and most divisive episodes in Canadian history. The Liberal Party of Sir Wilfrid Laurier split over compulsory service, and many of its senior members joined Borden in a Unionist coalition government to win the war through a maximum effort. The resulting 1917 election was a racist, venomous affair, with all sides appropriating patriotic slander to advance their cause. In order to win, prior to dissolving Parliament, Borden gave the vote to soldiers overseas, and also to the wives, mothers and sisters of soldiers, and to women in the military but took it away

from "enemy aliens" naturalized after 1902. Quebec was the only province not to vote Unionist, but, without considering the thousands of soldiers who voted for Borden, the margin of victory for the Unionists among civilian voters was merely one hundred thousand votes.

Partisanship in the midst of war tended to enrage the soldiers at the front. They believed for the most part that their sacrifices were necessary to preserve the freedoms most Canadians enjoyed, and the war made sense to them only if the beneficiaries of their efforts at home also worked for the common cause. The trenches boasted their fair share of political activists—Ralph Gibson Adams, a cyclist who later retrained as a pilot, referred to Laurier as "that old reprobate"—but it was important for the soldiers to know that everything possible was being done to help them win the war and go home. Major Alexander Anderson, writing to his father in September 1917, hoped that after enacting conscription the government would not shilly-shally in rounding up the troops. "I should think they could raise a few battalions in Ottawa alone, from unnecessary civil servants."

After the armistice, many veterans, including thousands who joined unions, protest movements and mainstream political parties, believed fundamentally that Canadian society had not appreciated their battlefield service and that life had gone on at home pretty much as normal while they were away. The difficulties that some veterans encountered in finding work after the war only aggravated this disappointment. For many

CANVAS OF WAR

facing page:

Alfred Bastien (1873–1955)

Canadian Gunners in the Mud,
Passchendaele, 1917
Oil on canvas
61.3 × 86.5 cm · CWM 8095

Belgian artist Alfred Bastien had just
begun working for the Canadian War
Memorials Fund when, on October 26,
1917, General Currie led the Canadian
Corps into the mud for which Passchendaele is now notorious. Lieutenant
Brooke Ferrar Gossage, serving with the
66th Battery, wrote in his diary: "New
Bty position an awful mud hole simply
covered with mud all the time and generally wet." By November 7, with losses
numbering over fifteen thousand,
Passchendaele was secure. Bastien has
depicted a group of gunners struggling to
release one of their guns from the mud.
The focus on the gun, rather than on
the soldiers, underlines the importance
of this weapon to success on the
battlefield.

left:

Frederick Etchells (1886–1973)

Armistice Day, Munitions Centre, c. 1918
Oil and blue crayon on canvas
304.1 × 238.7 cm · CWM 8154

English painter Frederick Etchells
practised primarily as an architect. Like
a number of artists of his time, however,
he was associated with the avant-garde
Vorticist group, itself influenced by
the Italian Futurist movement.
For these artists, the machine age—
as represented by the technology of
war—was the future.

returned men and their families, post-war Canada was definitely not "a land fit for heroes," as wartime propaganda had so earnestly predicted.

But it was not as though Canada forgot its men in uniform during the long years of struggle. Despite the social divisions occasioned or exacerbated by the war, for most Canadians the war was a profound national and personal experience, perhaps even a crusade, whose successful conclusion was just, honourable and necessary. "We just felt we had to get our shoulder to the wheel and get down to business," remembered Elaine Nelson who worked in a Toronto munitions factory. "There was everybody, every single class, from the squire's lady to Judy O'Grady and some few shades lower than Judy."[18] "Keeping faith" with those at the front was not just a standard cant in government propaganda but the attitude most Canadians expected. "There's nothing that draws people together more than mutual trouble," Nelson recalled, remembering the columns of death notices in the newspapers. "The boys are doing that for us, what are we doing for them? You just rolled up your sleeves and you didn't care how tired you were or anything else."[19] Thus, while soldiers enlisted for the duration of hostilities and saw no leave in Canada during the war, the nation worked hard to support their exertions in whatever small way possible.

Letters and parcels from home, newspapers, travelling lecturers, entertainment troupes and occasional visitors from Canada boosted morale and helped maintain the psychological link between soldiers and their families. Charities and local aid societies that organized drives to send mittens, socks, treats and foodstuffs to "our boys" not only provided welcome gifts but bolstered the men's mental and physical health. In a wet, sodden, disease-infested trench, a pair of fresh socks and a letter from home could make the difference between a casualty and an effective soldier. "I mustn't forget to thank you for the real touch of Canada you sent me— the maple leafs [sic]," wrote Ralph Gibson Adams to his mother on October 28, 1917, as the Canadian Corps battled up Passchendaele ridge. "I thought at once of those red maples down by Uncle John's before I read the letter. 'What are you going to do with them' some lads asked. 'Well' I answered 'first I'm going to kiss them' and I did."

Most soldiers beseeched their friends and families for letters and news, especially from wives, parents and girlfriends. The tidings were not always good. Family deaths, financial catastrophes and, perhaps worst of all, Dear John letters were an all-too-common occurrence. Most often, however, the letters brought personal words of encouragement from a wife or a sibling, or fond wishes from a proud child or a worried mother to soothe the lonely, miserable, frightened troops. The smallest word or comfort was eagerly received. "How can I thank you enough for the socks you sent me?" Basil Morris, a young officer in a tunnelling company, wrote to his sister Grace on May 12, 1916. "I will be dreaming socks for the next week or two."[20] The importance of the nation's support for its soldiers at the front cannot be overestimated.

James Morrice (1865–1924)
Canadians in the Snow, 1918
Oil on canvas
274.8 × 365.7 cm · CWM 8949

This painting by Canadian impressionist artist James Morrice is unusual because of its immense size. His reputation rests on smaller works that are more intimate in scale.

facing page:

Alfred Munnings (1878–1959)

Charge of Flowerdew's Squadron, c. 1918
Oil on canvas
50.8 × 61.5 cm · CWM 8571

Lieutenant G. M. Flowerdew, Lord Strathcona's Horse, was posthumously awarded the Victoria Cross for this action at Moreuil Wood on March 30, 1918. Nearly three-quarters of the Canadian cavalrymen were killed or wounded in the valiant attack, but it did help to stop Germany's last—and dangerously successful—offensive of the war.

left:

Leonard Richmond (1878–1965)

A Chinese Coolie, 1918
Pastel on brown paper
44.5 × 34.0 cm · CWM 8716

The Canadian Overseas Railway Construction Corps was the first unit of its kind to go overseas on active service beginning early in 1915. The nation's railway building prowess was critical to the maintenance of effective troop and supply movements. Nonetheless, the Canadians relied heavily on labourers from China provided by the Chinese Labour Force of the British Expeditionary Force. Leonard Richmond, an English artist, used pastels to make preparatory sketches in the field of railways under construction in France.

C. R. W. Nevinson (1889–1946)

War in the Air, 1918

Oil on canvas

304.8 × 243.8 cm · CWM 8651

C. R. W. Nevinson initially saw war as an ambulance driver and mechanic on the Flanders front. In July 1917 he became an official war artist working primarily for the British. "All my work," he wrote, "had to be done from rapid shorthand sketches made often under trying conditions in the front line, behind the lines, above the lines in observation balloons, over the lines in aeroplanes."

War in the Air proved a difficult assignment for the already exhausted artist. The stress of painting a reconstruction of an aerial battle involving celebrated Canadian flying ace Billy Bishop finally brought about a nervous breakdown. Lord Beaverbrook suggested he turn to painting "tiny sketches," but Nevinson declined. "He dismissed me good-naturedly as another damn-fool artist who failed to appreciate what he was offering, and told me that [Sir William] Orpen was the only artist who understood business."

Members of the Canadian Corps were not alone in facing such trials. Of the 619,636 Canadians who served in the Canadian Expeditionary Force (425,000 of them overseas), thousands served outside the Canadian Corps in both combat and support units in Canada, Britain and France. In the Canadian Army Medical Corps, 3141 nursing sisters, including 2504 who served with great distinction abroad, provided essential support services to the all-male military. Another 9600 Canadians enlisted in the navy and a further 22,812 in the British flying services, many of whom had first served in the CEF. Several of the latter, such as Lieutenant-Colonel W. A. Bishop, Lieutenant-Colonel Raymond Collishaw, Major D. R. MacLaren and Lieutenant-Colonel W. G. Barker, were among the war's leading air aces. Bishop was credited with seventy-two kills. Newfoundland, which was then not part of Canada (it joined in 1949), sent more than 8000 men to war, an enormous number given its pre-war population of roughly 250,000. Of the 6179 members of the Royal Newfoundland Regiment, 3619, or more than half, became casualties, including 1305 who died.

TO THE BITTER END

After Vimy, the Canadian Corps marched from one bloody victory to another. Building upon the lessons learned in earlier battles and the sound training and leadership provided by Sir Julian Byng and Sir Arthur Currie, the corps became possibly the finest fighting formation on the western front. At Passchendaele in late 1917, Currie warned his British superiors that German

positions atop a long, low ridge that had withstood numerous previous attacks could be captured, but not without sixteen thousand Canadian casualties. Field Marshal Sir Douglas Haig, overall commander of British forces in France, ordered him to proceed. After carefully preparing his attack, Currie struck in several phases beginning on October 26. Two weeks and 15,654 casualties later, the exhausted Canadians took command of the ridge. It was one of the most brutal battles in all of military history, with the troops advancing in dreadful weather across a rain-soaked, muddy valley to attack the German pillboxes, strong points and machine guns beyond. "In a flooded trench, the bloated bodies of some German soldiers are floating," noted Arthur Lapointe, a signaller with the 22nd Battalion, in his diary for November 5. "Here and there, too, arms and legs of dead men stick out from the mud, and awful faces appear, blackened by days and weeks under the beating sun. I try to turn from these dreadful sights, but wherever I look dead bodies emerge, shapelessly, from their shrouds of mud. . . . It would seem that life could never return to these fields of abundant death."[21]

During the winter of 1917–18, the Canadian Corps trained and recuperated from Passchendaele in a relatively quiet sector of the front. Normal "wastage" still cost more than thirty-five hundred casualties from December 1917 to March 1918, but the corps was fortunate in escaping the brunt of a series of German offensives, beginning in early March, that came close to winning the war. Although Canadian units plugged gaps

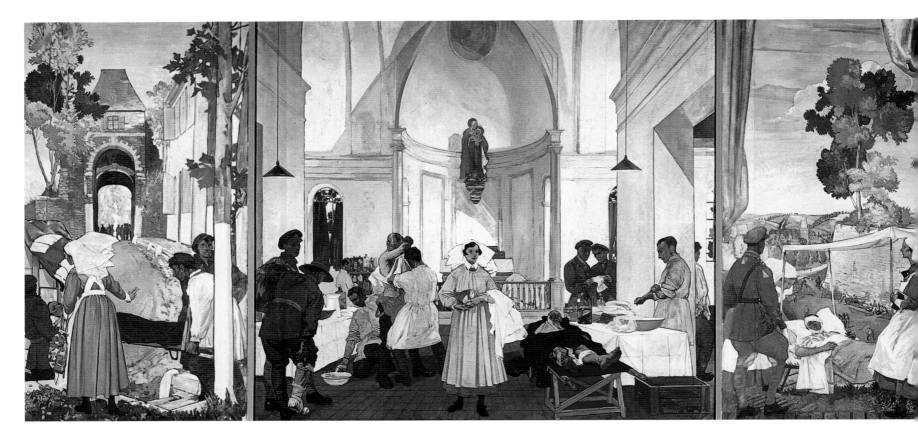

above:

Gerald Moira (1867–1959)

*No. 3 Canadian Stationary Hospital
at Doullens,* 1918

Oil on canvas

304.8 × 167.7 cm, 304.8 × 435.2 cm,
304.8 × 167.7 cm · CWM 8555, 8556, 8557

After seven months in Boulogne, No. 3
Stationary Hospital was sent to Doullens,
north of Amiens, in late 1916. It was
housed in a fifteenth-century citadel
outside the town, well away from
military and railway installations for
fear of bombing attacks such as the
one that later severely damaged No. 7
Canadian General Hospital at Étaples.
During the Allied retreat in the spring
of 1918, the hospital was very active.
It was bombed on the last two days of
May, and two surgeons, three nursing
sisters, four patients and sixteen
orderlies were killed.

facing page:

George Clausen (1852–1944)

Returning to the Reconquered Land, 1919

Oil on canvas

270.7 × 391.2 cm · CWM 8135

London-born George Clausen was
influenced by that great French painter
of peasant life, Jules Bastien-Lepage,
which is likely why he was offered
this commission. Late March 1918 saw
Clausen in France making studies, and
he completed this exceptionally large
painting by the end of that year.

in the Allied line, fought several short, sharp actions and suffered over nine thousand casualties between March and late July, the corps avoided the worst fighting. In August 1918, it was perhaps the best rested and most powerful fighting formation in the Allied order of battle. As the British, French and American armies went over to the attack, the Canadians were set to assume a critical role in the final stages of the war.

Between August 8 and November 11, 1918, when a general armistice came into effect, the Canadians on the western front repeatedly spearheaded a series of Allied offensives that broke the back of the German army. It was no accident that the Canadians played such a vital role. With excellent leadership, sound training, thorough preparation and battle experience, the Canadian Corps—called by one historian the "shock army of the British Empire"[22]—routinely assumed the most difficult objectives in the attack and, equally routinely, seized them.

The fighting in this last Hundred Days was far different from the trench deadlock that had typified the war since 1915. Although Allied generals had long dreamed of piercing the enemy's lines to restore movement and manoeuvre to the battlefield, only the German offensives in early 1918 succeeded in breaking the stalemate. Using specially trained stormtroops, surprise attacks and "fire and movement" tactics to suppress and avoid enemy strongpoints during a rapid advance, Germany achieved large territorial gains and sent Allied armies reeling in retreat from Flanders

in the north to the Marne River in the south. Canadian and other Allied armies had also been training for open warfare, or a war of manoeuvre freed from the trench deadlock, but Germany's successes provided many more valuable lessons. Germany's failure to turn its huge gains into a knockout blow, however, left its armies weakened and overextended.

On August 8, the Canadians, their movements carefully concealed because the Germans identified them as an elite attacking formation, led the counter-offensive at Amiens. It was a brilliant success. The attackers "broke right out into open fighting right away and instead of going forward in yards as they did in these other offensives, they went forward in miles," recalled C. B. Price, an officer in the 14th Battalion (Royal Montreal Regiment). "That was the best executed and the best picked out plan that was ever pulled off," said Private S. J. Car, 10th Battalion.[23]

Within days, even the successful Amiens offensive slowed down, but from that point forward Allied forces never lost the momentum. A hundred days later, Canadian troops entered Mons, Belgium, where they suffered their last battle casualty of the war, an infantryman shot by a German sniper just seconds before the armistice took effect on November 11. It was the most spectacular series of victories in Canadian military history, and also the most costly. Using aircraft, tanks, close infantry-artillery co-operation, innovative tactics, surprise and camouflage to good advantage, the confident Canadians ploughed through a

Alfred Bastien (1873–1955)
Over the Top, Neuville-Vitasse, 1918
Oil on canvas
140.5 × 229.6 cm · CWM 8058

Alfred Bastien served in the Belgian Army from 1915. Designated an official artist in 1916, he was placed at the disposal of the Canadian War Records Office in October 1917 and assigned to paint for the Canadian War Memorials Fund. Most of his time was spent with the French-speaking 22nd Battalion, Canadian Expeditionary Force, one result of which was *Over the Top, Neuville-Vitasse*. Neuville-Vitasse, located just south of Arras, was the site of heavy fighting in 1918.

CANVAS OF WAR

facing page:

Inglis Sheldon-Williams (1870–1940)
The Return to Mons, 1920
Oil on canvas
302.3 × 452.0 cm · CWM 8969

Inglis Sheldon-Williams was appointed a Canadian war artist in December 1917 but did not receive a pass to go to the front until October 1918. The experience moved him. "[It is] such a noble epic," he wrote to his wife. "It has nothing to do with studios and art talk. Whatever I do with my paints I have found and possessed this great thing—I would like to share it if I can." He painted two huge canvasses, of which this is one. Subsequently, he suffered a nervous breakdown.

left:

Thurstan Topham (1888–1966)
A Tank in Action, c. 1916
Charcoal on paper
25.9 × 35.3 cm · CWM 8898

Thurstan Topham's studies of tanks are among the earliest painted records of this new weapon in action. The Second World War Canadian artist Campbell Tinning saw some of Topham's work for the first time in a 1991 exhibition at the Canadian War Museum. "I was suitably humbled by the inclusion of some work by Thurstan Topham who I met in 1939 at the Arts Club in Montreal and thought a dull old boy—little, did I know—little did I know."

series of strong German defences, taking thousands of prisoners in the process. General Erich Ludendorff, quartermaster general of the German army, called the Canadian-led breakthrough on August 8 "the black day of the German army."

Even after the long struggle, or perhaps because of it, the war's memory would be carefully preserved as a "good" fight, even a righteous one. Poets, scholars and a few learned veterans would later pronounce on the futility of it all, but they would be a distinct minority in post-war Canada. Veterans and their families preferred to recall the purpose of their sacrifice. The First World War was a formative experience for Canada. Almost every facet of Canadian life had been transformed by the war years. Some changes, such as personal income tax and widespread federal programs for war veterans, were there to stay; others, such as male-dominated society's acceptance of large numbers of married women in the workplace, proved temporary. Canada emerged from the war as a major military power with an unparalleled record of battlefield success, yet in the post-war period the country would shrink from international obligations into near isolationism. Its victorious armed forces would wither under the combined weight of economic catastrophe, public disinterest and a profound fear lest military commitments reaggravate the social and political cleavages occasioned by the war. Most Canadians felt justifiably proud of the country's achievements in the struggle, but the sight of disabled or unemployed veterans reminded all Canadians that international

prominence and martial success had a steep price. The altered political landscape, with the Conservative Party largely ejected from Quebec because of its stand on conscription and a series of strengthened regional protest parties on the Prairies and elsewhere, was a further caution that entanglements abroad had costs at home. Canada would not refuse, in some future crisis, to march into battle with its closest friends and allies, especially Britain, but far fewer Canadians would welcome it with the same enthusiasm they had in the summer of 1914.

In the trenches, barracks, aerodromes and warships, November 11, 1918, was far too soon to reflect upon such meaning. Exhausted Canadians welcomed the news of the ceasefire and hoped desperately that it would last. At Mons, civilian exuberance seemed strangely at odds with the footsore Canadians who trudged through the town and beyond to take up new positions for possibly one more advance. "When our arms were finally victorious," remembered air ace Lieutenant-Colonel Raymond Collishaw, "it was difficult not to dwell with remorse upon the price of victory, and one wished that the most gallant of my contemporaries were present to participate in celebrating what their valour had helped to achieve." On the last day of the war, George Anderson, an infantryman from the Ottawa Valley, wrote to his family: "I suppose old Canada will be right up in the air by this time, and the old Prescott band will be in full swing. To tell the truth it seems hard to realize it, and that we are through with this awful slaughter."

Fred Varley (1881–1969)

German Prisoners, c. 1919

Oil on canvas

127.4 × 183.7 cm · CWM 8961

Future Group of Seven artist Fred Varley found mud a problem while working at the front during the fall of 1918. German planes flew overhead, and there was occasional shelling around his area. On September 16 he wrote to his wife: "I've just mapped out a canvas of a subject—the details having been gathered in spasms. All my notes up to the present are the slightest—no paintings—couldn't be done—I had to scoot *'avec vite'* from one of my horrors for the Hun took a fancy to the same place & chucked his shells right over."

Ernest Sampson (1887–1946)

Armistice Day, Toronto, c. 1918
Oil on canvas
152.8 × 91.7 cm · CWM 8795

Ernest Sampson, an influential poster
designer and printer, was instrumental
in producing works of Canadian art that
decorated barracks during the Second
World War, and also a series of Victory
Loan posters.

ENDNOTES

1   Sandra Gwyn, *Tapestry of War: A Private View of Canadians in the Great War* (Toronto: HarperCollins, 1992), p 50.

2   Ronald G. Haycock, *Sam Hughes: The Public Career of a Controversial Canadian, 1885–1916* (Waterloo, ON: Wilfrid Laurier University Press, 1986).

3   Cited in Jonathan F. Vance, *Death So Noble: Memory, Meaning, and the First World War* (Vancouver: University of British Columbia Press, 1997), p 35.

4   Louis Keene, *'Crumps': The Plain Story of a Canadian Who Went* (Boston: Houghton Mifflin, 1917), pp 5–6.

5   *Flanders' Fields* (CBC, 1964), episode 3, pp 14–16.

6   Keene, *'Crumps,'* p 13.

7   Victor N. Swanston, *Who Said War Is Hell!* (Saskatoon: Modern Press, 1983), p 10.

8   Arthur Hunt Chute, *The Real Front* (New York: Harper & Brothers, 1918), p 16.

9   *Flanders' Fields*, episode 5, p 15.

10 D. J. Goodspeed, *The Road Past Vimy: The Canadian Corps, 1914–1918* (Toronto: Macmillan, 1969), p 38.

11 Cited in Desmond Morton, *When Your Number's Up: The Canadian Soldier in the First World War* (Toronto: Random House, 1993), p 228.

12 Cited in Morton, *When Your Number's Up*, p 136.

13 Cited in Daphne Read, ed., *The Great War and Canadian Society: An Oral History* (Toronto: New Hogtown Press, 1978), p 141.

14 *Flanders' Fields*, episode 9, p 11.

15 Ibid., p 30.

16 Cited in Read, *The Great War*, p 192.

17 Cited in G. W. L. Nicholson, *Canadian Expeditionary Force, 1914–1919* (Ottawa: Queen's Printer, 1962), pp 342–43.

18 Read, *The Great War*, p 156.

19 Ibid., p 157.

20 Grace Morris Craig, *But This Is Our War* (Toronto: University of Toronto Press, 1981), p 66.

21 Arthur Lapointe, *Soldier of Quebec (1916–1919)*, trans. by R. C. Fetherstonhaugh (Montreal: Editions Edouard Garand, 1931), pp 74–5.

22 Shane B. Schreiber, *Shock Army of the British Empire: The Canadian Corps in the Last 100 Days of the Great War* (Westport, CT: Praeger, 1997).

23 *Flanders' Fields*, episode 14, p 10.

THE FACE OF ARMAGEDDON

*Great nations write their autobiographies in three manu-
scripts: the book of their deeds, the book of their words,
and the book of their art. Not one of these books can be
understood unless we read the two others; but of the three
the only quite trustworthy one is the last.*

JOHN RUSKIN, ST. MARK'S REST

ON JANUARY 4, 1919, an exhibition of war art commissioned by the Canadian War Memorials Fund
opened at Burlington House, home of the Royal
Academy in London, England. One of the guests was
Kenneth Clark, later to become the director of Britain's
National Gallery. Seeing Canada's First World War
art for the first time that evening, he recalled decades
later, was the single most important influence on his
decision to initiate a Second World War art program
for Great Britain.

Like Clark, few of the Royal Academy's guests
could have anticipated what Burlington House had in
store. Its galleries displayed a world of carnage, courage
and comradeship, which just months before had been
an almost everyday reality across the English Channel in
France and Belgium. Those present at the opening that
day, including many of London's social and political
elite, were face to face with the most innovative, evocative and important art commission ever conceived in
wartime. And it was Canada's.

Politically, the story of Canada's First World War
art program, the Canadian War Memorials, is woven
through with tales of power and ambition. The diaries
and letters of the artists, however, tell a different
story, mainly of personal anguish in the presence of
so much death and desecration. Arriving in England,
the Canadian artists seemed lighthearted, writing of
drink, poker and the good life. By war's end, their
correspondence was infused with an awareness of the
conflict's influence both on themselves and on the
world around them.

Their art, too, moves uneasily between recording
battles, finding the essence in common experiences and
seeking relief in painting the remaining pastoral landscape. The war output of Newfoundland-born Maurice
Cullen clearly shows this tension. On one occasion, he
painted a bleak and profoundly disturbing picture of a
dead horse and rider, in which the very brushwork documents his agitation at the sight. It must have been with
relief that he turned to another canvas, and an impressionist style, to paint the picturesque Belgian town of
Huy, on the Meuse River, on a sunny day.

In part because of its very variety, the First World
War art collection of nearly one thousand works by over
one hundred artists, more than a third of whom are
Canadian, is a collection of international stature. Not
only does it illustrate, commemorate and illuminate the
major events of the First World War as experienced by
Canadians, but it also forms a major building block in
the development of Canadian art. Much of the familiar

Richard Jack (1866–1952)
The Second Battle of Ypres,
22 April to 25 May 1915, 1917
Oil on canvas
371.5 × 589.0 cm · CWM 8179

The first commission completed for the Canadian War Memorials Fund (CWMF), *The Second Battle of Ypres* is also one of the biggest. It commemorates the first major action of Canadian troops at the front, which led British Field Marshal Sir John French to declare that the Canadians "saved the situation." Sir Edmund Walker, of the CWMF's Advisory Arts Council in Canada, doubted that Jack's painting captured the achievement in a way Canadians would understand: "Whatever its merits, the public of the future is not likely to appreciate such realistic treatment of war." British-born Richard Jack moved to Canada in 1930.

facing page:

Maurice Cullen (1866–1934)

Dead Horse and Rider in a Trench, 1918

Oil on canvas

112.0 × 143.0 cm · CWM 8140

Along with Fred Varley, William Beatty and Charles Simpson, the Newfoundland-born Maurice Cullen was one of the first official war artists appointed by the Canadian War Memorials Fund.

In a May 3, 1918, letter to his wife, Maud, Varley described Cullen at Seaford Camp on the south coast of England, before both artists crossed to France. "He's a plucky man, you know, taking on this work at 52, and as simple as a little child. He is not intellectual, far from it. He loves twilight and mysteries and is a fiend for cigarettes. . . . He likes comfort, does not work half as hard as he should, and chooses his position out of the wind etc., where he can rig up a sketch stool, light a cigarette, paint and carry on a conversation."

landscape painting of the Group of Seven, for example, owes its genesis to sights seen and recorded in the mud and the trenches of the western front.

The Canadian War Memorials collection was the brainchild of Sir Max Aitken, later Lord Beaverbrook, who had no particular association with the pre-war art world. Born in 1879 in Ontario, this slight, energetic and charismatic "son of the manse" made an early fortune in the young dominion, although his aggressive business methods earned him accolades and suspicion in nearly equal measure. After relocating to Britain, the millionaire moved easily into its highest aristocratic and political circles. He became financially involved in 1911 with the *Daily Express* and bought it outright five years later, using the respected newspaper to expand his influence. Always a Canadian at heart, Aitken decided in 1916 to initiate and personally oversee a project, through the Canadian War Records Office, to record the war from Canada's point of view.

Aitken's media interests made him ideally suited to the task of documenting the war in film, photograph and print. His experience with a mass circulation daily newspaper meant that he also knew what engaged people's interests. A single event convinced him of the need to record the war on canvas: the horrific German gas attack on the Canadians at the Second Battle of Ypres in April and May 1915.

For a variety of reasons the battle was not photographed, so, in November 1916, Aitken commissioned through his new organization, the Canadian War Memorials Fund, a huge 3.7-by-5.9-metre painting from British society artist Richard Jack. Aitken liked the work, although it was subsequently scorned by generations of art historians for both its traditional style and its historical inaccuracy. Undoubtedly this venture's success, combined with the knowledge that the lifespan of photographs was just twenty-five years, contributed to his decision to commission more artists to record Canada's war experiences for posterity. His new fund, after all, sought to provide "suitable Memorials in the form of Tablets, Oil Paintings, etc. to the Canadian Heroes and Heroines of the War."

Although Aitken's views on art are not well documented, those of the man he hired as his war art adviser certainly are. In his essay for the lavishly illustrated book, *Art and War*, that accompanied the Burlington House exhibition, Hungarian-born art critic Paul Konody wrote that art has a unique ability to record, commemorate and memorialize. With Konody's advice, and help from a committed group of newspaper owners and influential Britons such as Lord Rothermere, Aitken's war art program definitely had panache.

He and Konody worked essentially from two angles. First, they continued to think in terms of major commissions, or big pictures. Aitken, created Lord Beaverbrook in December 1916, first thought that the oversized works might help decorate the new Houses of Parliament in Ottawa, the original buildings having been largely destroyed by fire in 1916. Secondly, they agreed that artists should spend time on the battlefield making sketches

Maurice Cullen (1866–1934)
Huy on the Meuse,
on the Road to the Rhine, c. 1919
Oil on canvas
143.0 × 178.0 cm · CWM 8148

So many of Maurice Cullen's works are grim that *Huy on the Meuse,* looking so much like one of his favourite subjects, Quebec City, must have been a relief to paint. The artist has chosen to work in an impressionist style that allows him to capture in paint the fleeting effects of sun on snow and the soft quality of smoke rising from the tiny steamer in the river. As an artist, Cullen was of critical importance to late nineteenth-century Canadian art in introducing the methods of the French Impressionist painters.

facing page:

Alfred Munnings (1878–1959)
Captain Prince Antoine of Orléans and Braganza, c. 1918
Oil on canvas
50.3 × 61.0 cm · CWM 8574

War artist Sir William Orpen met Alfred Munnings in France and published an account of his fellow painter at work. At the time, Munnings was preparing a portrait of Prince Antoine of Orleans and Braganza, aide-de-camp to General Seely, the commanding officer of the Canadian Cavalry Brigade. "He used to make the poor Prince sit all day, circumnavigating the château as the sun went round. I remember going out one morning and seeing the Prince sitting upon his horse, as good as gold. Munnings was chewing a straw when I came up to them. 'Here,' said he. 'You're just the fellow I want. What colour is that reflected light under the horse's belly?' 'Very warm yellow,' said I. 'There! I told you so,' said he to the Prince. Apparently there had been some argument over the matter. Anyway, he mixed a full brush of warm yellow and laid it on. Just before lunch I came out again. There they were in another spot. 'Hey!' said Munnings, 'come here. What colour is the reflection now?' 'Bright violet,' said I. 'There! What did I tell you?' said he to the Prince; and he mixed a brush-load of bright violet, and laid it on.

"As the sun was sinking I went out again, and there was the poor Prince, still in the saddle. Munnings had nearly as much paint on himself as on the canvas. He was very excited. I could see him gesticulating from a distance. When he saw me he called out: 'Come here quickly before the light goes. What colour is the reflection on the horse's belly now?' 'Bright green,' said I. 'It is,' said he, 'and the Prince won't believe me.' And he quickly made a heap of bright green and plastered it over the bright yellow and bright violet reflections of the morning and midday. So ended the day's work, and the bright green remained in full view till the next sitting."

top left:
Lord Beaverbrook (c. 1917–1919)
National Archives of Canada PA 006477

bottom left:
Sir Edmund Walker
Photo by Sidney Carter
National Archives of Canada PA 124323

of archival value, which might ultimately be turned into larger works. Alfred Munnings, for example, was attached to both the Canadian Cavalry Corps and the Canadian Forestry Corps with this thought in mind.

The scant surviving records seem to indicate that there was little planning regarding the selection of artists. Some of those identified were personal friends of Beaverbrook's, or had been brought to his attention; others were establishment figures in both the British and the Canadian art worlds. Depending on their reputation, skills and availability, artists were asked to complete specific commissions for larger paintings or were dispatched overseas for predetermined time periods to sketch in the field. Four of the Canadian artists (Fred Varley, William Beatty, Maurice Cullen and Charles Simpson) were given official status together with the rank and pay of an army captain. Of the remainder, a few were, or had been, serving soldiers who liked to paint or newspaper illustrators who sought another market for their work.

Smaller-scale paintings were emerging from the program, but Beaverbrook's special interest in size and impact brought him into conflict with officials in Ottawa, especially at the National Gallery of Canada. The main player, Sir Edmund Walker, chairman of the gallery's board of trustees, was an extraordinarily effective man who had risen from bank clerk to president of the Canadian Bank of Commerce. His interests and acquaintances were wide, and his dedication to Canada's cultural, intellectual and business life,

legendary. Working with him at the gallery was the Englishman Eric Brown, its first director. Brown's deep affection for his adopted country's wilderness, which manifested itself in regular camping trips, led to a strong and deep personal and professional association with the painters of the Group of Seven.

Ensuring that the war art program truly reflected Canada's role in the conflict was of critical concern to both Walker and Brown. Although they appreciated Beaverbrook's extraordinary drive in founding and funding the Canadian war art program, they had different views on what form the record should take. Gallery officials were interested in field study, not grand studio composition. They also worried that the program recommended too many commissions for British artists. Such nationalist sympathies were hardly unique. Although Canadians were still British subjects, many craved an identity, in politics and in art, that would be distinct from the Mother Country. Acknowledging this sentiment, Prime Minister Sir Robert Borden tried to ensure that the Canadian Corps was recognized as a national army under Canadian control.

Walker asked Beaverbrook to employ Canadian artists. Beaverbrook was receptive and gradually hired more Canadians. One of the first was A.Y. Jackson, in later years a leading figure in the Group of Seven and in Canadian art generally. Jackson, who had been wounded early in the war and met Beaverbrook while convalescing, spent two periods on the western front, producing an important body of Canadian work. His cheerful

Arthur Lismer (1885–1969)

Olympic *with Returned Soldiers*, 1919

Oil on canvas

123.1 × 163.1 cm · CWM 8363

Arthur Lismer, a future member of the Group of Seven, was principal of the Victoria School of Art and Design when he heard that Canadian artists were being hired by the Canadian War Memorials Fund. He came up with his own suggestion. "What I would like to secure is permission to gather material here in Halifax. More than any other city perhaps in the Dominion Halifax is of vital interest as a war city and there is a tremendous amount of activity that I'd like to record—the departure & arrival of troopships, convoys, hospital ships, troopships from Australia & New Zealand, & the States—camouflaged men of war of different nationalities—it's intensely interesting and graphic & no one is painting it." Later he wrote, "The 'Olympic' which has carried so many of the Canadians over, docked here last week. It was a magnificent sight—& is the most typical of all such subjects."

CANVAS OF WAR

A.Y. Jackson (1882–1974)

A Copse, Evening, 1918
Oil on canvas
86.8 × 111.8 cm · CWM 8204

The most significant of all A.Y. Jackson's war paintings, *A Copse, Evening* is hugely indebted to the example of the English war artist Paul Nash, whom the Canadian artist greatly admired. On viewing it for the first time, Canadian art critic Barker Fairley wrote: "This must be one of the most enduring pictures in the collection. . . . It owes its success to . . . its glacial light prospect . . . a phosphorescent beauty and almost a fascination that yet in no way detracts from the grimness of the conception."

left:

A.Y. Jackson (1882–1974)

Gas Attack, Liévin, 1918
Oil on canvas
63.6 × 77.0 cm · CWM 8197

In a 1953 article in *Canadian Art*, A.Y. Jackson wrote: "I went with Augustus John one night to see a gas attack we made on the German lines. It was like a wonderful display of fireworks, with our clouds of gas and the German flares and rockets of all colours."

reaction to the front when he returned as an artist—"same old war, . . . same old soldiers sticking it out, fed up but cheerful and doing impossible things, same old mud and shell holes"—belies the content of many of his paintings. The title of *A Copse, Evening* adds ironic twist to the devastation depicted by the work. Silhouetted against a searchlight-covered sky, the copse is, quite clearly, no more.

How Jackson worked and what he produced provide insight into the nature of Canada's First World War art. He drew quickly, in pencil, in small sketchbooks that he carried with him while moving through the countryside. Sometimes a sketch took up a whole page; at other times, several very small drawings fit on a single sheet, each framed by a rectangular line. Sometimes he used coloured pencil and graphite; at other times he noted the colours of the scene he was sketching in tiny, hand-written comments alongside or in the drawing itself. On most drawings, he carefully recorded the date.

Jackson also appears to have had the time to sketch outdoors in oil on board, a painting method favoured by many of the Canadian artists. The degree to which he used this method is unknown as he was not required to hand in any of these small studies to Beaverbrook's team. As a result, these works remain scattered in private and public collections. The oil sketches and the finished paintings that resulted from them show that Jackson made several studies of different views from a single location. Back in his London studio, the artist worked up the drafts into finished compositions.

Other artists influenced Jackson's work, especially one British painter and printmaker who was also an employee of the Canadian program. Paul Nash's vivid and harsh portrayals of the western front challenged Jackson's abilities as a landscape painter. In particular, in Nash's use of the destroyed tree trunk, Jackson found an emblem of war's destructiveness to incorporate in his own art. This extraordinarily meaningful war symbol later was absorbed into the post-war Canadian landscape tradition: the stark tree trunks of Group of Seven member Lawren Harris's Lake Superior landscapes are among its finest examples.

Walker was also instrumental in ensuring official commissions for several other Canadian artists. Fred Varley, another future member of the Group of Seven, was attached to the Canadian Corps. He joined the troops in August 1918 as they advanced rapidly from Amiens, France, to Mons, Belgium, in the last Allied offensive of the war, known as the Hundred Days. Varley wrote of the terrible campaign to his wife, Maud:

> You in Canada . . . cannot realize at all what war is like. You must see it and live it. You must see the barren deserts war has made of once fertile country . . . see the turned up graves, see the dead on the field, freakishly mutilated—headless, legless, stomachless, a perfect body and a passive face and a broken empty skull—see your own countrymen, unidentified, thrown into a cart, their coats over them, boys digging a grave in a land of yellow slimy mud and green pools of water under a weeping sky. You must have heard

Mabel May (1877–1971)
Women Making Shells, 1919
Oil on canvas
182.7 × 214.9 cm · CWM 8409

Mabel May was invited to paint a home-front composition by Eric Brown, director of the National Gallery and an active participant, with Sir Edmund Walker, in the employment of Canadian artists for the Canadian War Memorials Fund. "As you may know," he wrote, "the Canadian War Records is getting work done in Canada now, and several artists are working on some of the most interesting subjects connected with the war. . . . I have wondered whether you have seen anything of women's work in munition factories or aeroplane works that has struck you as a good subject for a picture! I remember work of yours which should make such a subject easy and interesting to you, and I should be very glad if you would let me know what you think of the matter or if it was worth while [sic] coming up here about it, to come and discuss the matter any time convenient to you. The way to manage the matter would be to decide on your subject or subjects and their size, which should not be small, six feet or so, and then suggest a price that would cover your studies and the finished picture. I would then formally commission the picture and you would go ahead."

CANVAS OF WAR

facing page:

Fred Varley (1881–1969)
Some Day the People Will Return, 1918
Oil on canvas
182.9 × 228.6 cm · CWM 8910

In an April 1919 letter to his friend and fellow Canadian artist Arthur Lismer, Fred Varley wrote: "I was in Ypres the other day—in Maple Copse and Sanctuary Wood—you pass places such as Piccadilly or Hell Fire Corner and you follow up a plank road and then cut off over a festering ground, walking on the tips of shell holes which are filled with dark and unholy water. You pass over swamps on rotting duckboards, past bleached bones of horses with their harness still on, past violated rude crosses sticking up from the filth and the stink of decay is flung over all. There was a lovely wood there once with a stream running thro' it but now the trees are powdered up and mingle with the soil. One or two silly maimed stumps are left, ghostly mockeries of what they were.

"I tell you Arthur, your wildest nightmares pale before reality. How the devil one can paint anything to express such is beyond me. The story of War is told in the thousand and one things that mingle with the earth—equipment, bits of clothing almost unrecognizable, an old boot stuck up from a mound of filth, a remnant of sock inside, and inside that—well, I slightly released the boot, it came away in my hand and the bones sifted out of the sodden rag like fine sand. Ashes to ashes, dust to dust. I find myself marvelling over the metamorphosis from chrysalis to butterfly but I never get beyond marvelling."

left:
Portrait of Fred Varley in uniform (c. 1918). Fred Varley, one of Canada's first four official war artists, had no idea what he would find in France, and his first letter home gives no hint of the despair he would later communicate. Writing in the music room on board the Royal Mail Steamer *Grampian,* in the company of his three fellow official war artists, he noted: "[William] Beatty's playing his head off at poker. [Charles] Simpson & [Maurice] Cullen are sitting back trying to enjoy this delicious music and I, well, I enjoy all the bally lot. . . ."
Original photo courtesy of the late Maud Varley, Vancouver · National Gallery of Canada

the screeching shells and have the shrapnel fall
around you, whistling by you—Seen the results of it,
seen scores of horses, bits of horses lying around in
the open—in the street and soldiers marching by
these scenes as if they never knew of their presence—
until you've lived this . . . you cannot know.

He memorialized what he saw in some of the most moving, bleak and starkly vivid works to come out of the war.

More than anyone else, Walker and Brown were
responsible for including two aspects of the war in its
artistic record: the home front and women. Future
Group of Seven member Arthur Lismer created memorable images of Halifax, Nova Scotia, in wartime, producing vibrant portraits of dazzle-painted ships in the
harbour. In addition, Frank Johnston, another Group of
Seven artist, worked for several months documenting
pilot training at various bases in Ontario. His watercolours of Curtiss JN-4 aircraft joyously looping-the-loop
above the tranquil fall farm landscape uniquely convey
the idea of flight and show that for some members of the
Royal Flying Corps, war was not entirely a grim business.

For the most part, women artists were given women's
work as subjects, but during the war that work itself
evolved as hundreds of thousands of women performed
tasks usually dominated by men. Mabel May, a
Montreal artist, enthusiastically depicted women filling
shells, in a moving impressionist composition, and
Manly MacDonald composed a cheerful picture of
women hoeing in a field.

As the war drew to a close, Walker and a number of
senior government officials planned a special building
in Ottawa to house the art, artifacts and archival records
from the war. Simultaneously, Beaverbrook announced
his own commissioned designs for a monumental war
memorial art gallery, also to be built in the nation's
capital. A decade of lobbying by protagonists of both
schemes produced neither building. Instead, Beaverbrook lost interest in the project, feeling generally that
his wartime work for Canada had been underappreci-
ated. The National Gallery was left with the art. In 1971,
the gallery transferred the collection, along with the art
from the Second World War program, to the Canadian
War Museum, where it remains, as it has been since
1921, largely in storage.

Of course, none of these developments were fore-
cast on January 4, 1919. Instead, the well-heeled guests
mingled gracefully in their aristocratic surroundings,
lavishing praise on an extraordinary collection of paintings whose subtle hues and bold strokes conveyed so
well the nature of those catastrophic war years. That day
the guests saw that the artists had painted from their own
personal experiences the history of a generation. Like
the soldiers they depicted, many of the artists too had
seen comrades and brothers die. They had marched over
corpses, suffered through deafening bombardments and
endured inhumane conditions. Today, the survival of
these painters' work ensures for all Canadians a vivid,
first-hand account of "how it was."

Frank Johnston (1888–1949)
Looking into the Blue, 1918
Watercolour and gouache on board
57.5 × 72.1 cm · CWM 8267

Frank Johnston, a future member of the Group of Seven, was paid 250 dollars a month to make sketches in the Ontario flying training camps in late 1918. "While I was at Beamsville (The School of Aerial Gunnery)," he wrote, "I had some fine flights, and have done all the stunts that the flyers do—barring a crash."

In an unpublished autobiographical sketch, Johnston wrote: "Flying in a spiral upward, everytime, the plane turned upward and the great silver wings towered up on one side, and fell away on the other, I thought we were about to upset, but it always righted itself and higher ever higher we rose till the land below became a beautiful rug, with a somewhat geometric design, of all colours, broken by light ribbons, that were the main highways. Then we flew out over the lake, and here I began to make notes feverishly, and signalling as a subject suggested itself to me."

THE

SECOND

WORLD

WAR

THE SECOND CRUSADE

On no man was there a compulsion, save that which came from his own heart. Indeed there were grave reasons why most of them should have held back. But they were not that kind of men. Even as the volunteers had rallied from the counties to die at Ypres—so did they rally now.

FARLEY MOWAT, *THE REGIMENT*

IN SEPTEMBER 1939, the world went to war for the second time in a generation. Germany's invasion of Poland on September 1 finally convinced France and Britain that the territorial ambitions of German dictator Adolf Hitler could not be appeased. After Berlin refused to withdraw from Poland, Britain and France declared war on September 3. A week later, on September 10, Canada did the same. The week-long delay both symbolized Canadian independence from Britain and indicated Ottawa's intention to define carefully the terms of its own war effort.

The First World War had shown most Canadians that wars were bloody, costly and divisive, even when undertaken to defend friends, allies or democratic values. The Liberal Party of Sir Wilfrid Laurier, the Official Opposition in Parliament, had split badly in 1917 over the introduction of conscription for overseas military service. Heavy casualties in Canada's army overseas had led to a bruising political fight at home. Should Canada make every effort to keep its fighting forces up to

strength, even if it meant compelling men to go overseas? Or should voluntary efforts continue, even if fewer recruits meant reducing the size of Canada's military contribution? The Canadian Expeditionary Force had earned national honour and independence on the field of battle, but it had also created the conditions for disunity and conflict at home.

William Lyon Mackenzie King, a minister in Laurier's government from 1909 to 1911, learned much from the First World War's impact on Canada's domestic affairs. In any future war involving a direct threat to Britain, he knew that public opinion and his appraisal of Canada's national interest would guarantee Ottawa's support for London. But he also knew that how Canada participated might, in terms of domestic politics, be at least as important as whether it acted at all. In particular, he feared that, as in 1917, large numbers of ground troops overseas could entail heavy casualties that might, in turn, mean another national crisis over compulsory overseas service. In the First World War, this issue had pitted French Canada against English Canada in pitched political battles, which sometimes spilled over into the streets. The country still bore their scars.

As prime minister from late 1921 until 1930, and again from 1935 during the Great Depression, Mackenzie King was neither anti-British nor, necessarily, anti-war. He simply weighed the possibility of Canadian involvement in any future struggle against what he perceived as the likely domestic costs to his country, his party and his political future, and concluded that if Canada did

Orville Fisher (1911–1999)

Recruits Wanted, 1941

Watercolour and carbon pencil on art board

36.3 × 51.1 cm · CWM 12584

Orville Fisher enlisted in the Canadian Army in 1940 and worked as a service artist in Ottawa from February 1941 until April 1942. In 1943 he received his commission as an official war artist.

fight again, it must do so on its own terms. First, this would mean allowing Parliament to consider and decide on Canada's participation in any war, based on the constitutional independence afforded Canada (and Britain's other Dominions) by the Statute of Westminster (1931). Secondly, it would entail waging a struggle in which Canada substituted naval and air support and economic aid for large numbers of ground troops in an attempt to limit casualties, thereby avoiding conscription and a national unity quandary. To some Canadians, especially in the opposition Conservative Party (renamed the Progressive Conservative Party in 1942), this approach seemed the height of anti-British, isolationist nonsense; to others, it was shrewd, prudent politics.

Having lost more than sixty thousand lives in the First World War, a weary Canada demobilized its victorious army with almost indecent haste after 1918. The Royal Canadian Air Force (RCAF), created in 1924, and a reorganized Royal Canadian Navy (RCN) had since broadened the potential scope for Canadian military action in any future war but, by the late 1930s, Canada's half-million strong wartime armed forces had shrunk to roughly ten thousand regular personnel, including the air force and the navy. Fifty thousand or so poorly trained, poorly equipped reservists rounded out a military establishment that was grossly unprepared for what lay ahead. By 1938, Mackenzie King and many other Canadians had reluctantly concluded that aggressive dictators in Germany, Italy and Japan might not be appeased

indefinitely, but substantial increases in the defence budget and stiffening political resolve had not added much equipment or many troops by the outbreak of war.

In August 1939, Canadian forces mobilized in lock-step with their British counterparts, but Mackenzie King reacted angrily to the plan advanced by the army's general staff for a large expeditionary force. A direct appeal from Britain and public pressure to send troops nevertheless ensured that forces would be sent immediately. The 1st Canadian Infantry Division, some sixteen thousand men including support troops, began arriving in Britain in mid-December under the command of Major-General A. G. L. McNaughton, whom Mackenzie King had personally selected as a man with the intellectual gifts and sensibilities to ensure Canadian forces did not suffer unnecessary losses. At a meeting on December 7, just before the division's departure, the prime minister urged McNaughton to impress upon his troops that they were engaged in a great crusade as "defenders of the faith and of civilization against the domination of free countries by barbarism."[1] Many other Canadians shared this view and described their war as a religious quest. Leonard A. Costello, an RCAF chaplain during the war, later recalled that "when the cause of not only our civilization but even of Christianity was questioned there was no choice then to fight for what we knew to be right."

The prime minister's hope that Canada's war might be fought with few casualties and limited overseas commitments found its echo in Canadians' divided opinions

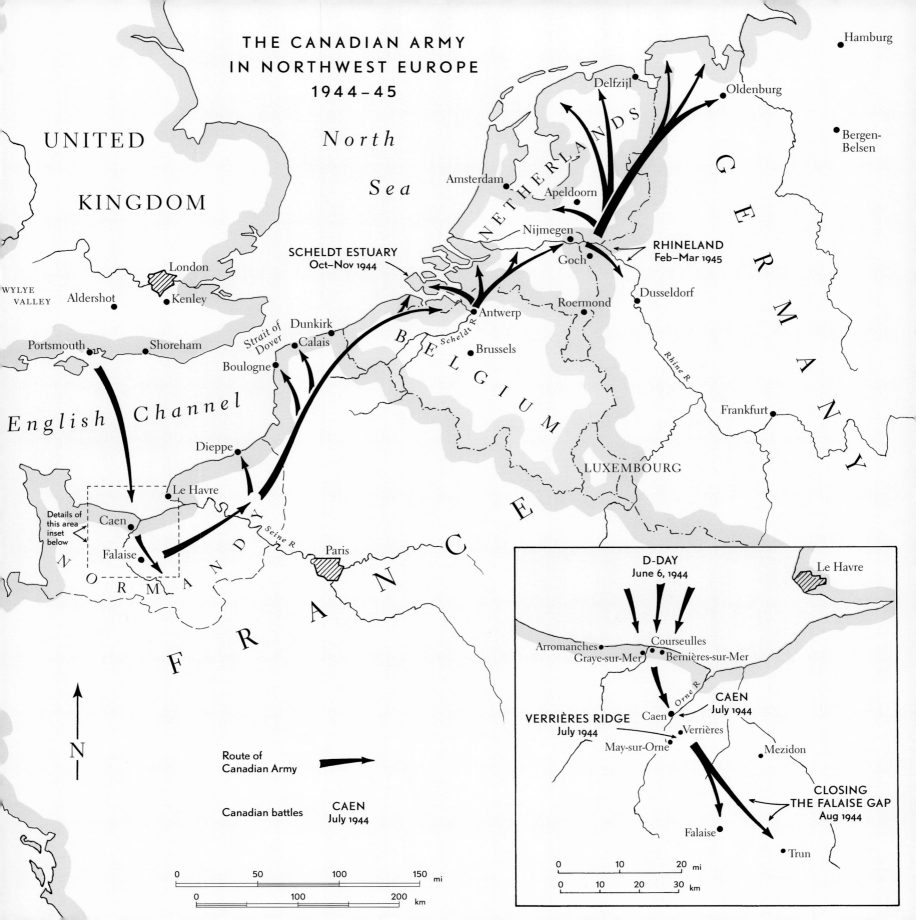

THE CANADIAN ARMY
IN NORTHWEST EUROPE
1944–45

UNITED

KINGDOM

North

Sea

WYLIE
VALLEY

London

Aldershot

Kenley

Portsmouth

Shoreham

Strait of Dover

Dunkirk

Calais

Boulogne

Dieppe

Le Havre

English Channel

Details of
this area
inset
below

Caen

Falaise

N O R M A N D Y

Seine R.

Paris

F R A N C E

SCHELDT ESTUARY
Oct–Nov 1944

Amsterdam

N E T H E R L A N D S

Delfzijl

Oldenburg

Apeldoorn

Nijmegen

Goch

RHINELAND
Feb–Mar 1945

Antwerp

Scheldt R.

B E L G I U M

Brussels

Roermond

Dusseldorf

LUXEMBOURG

Rhine R.

Frankfurt

G E R M A N Y

Hamburg

Bergen-
Belsen

Route of
Canadian Army

Canadian battles   CAEN
July 1944

N

0   50   100   150 mi

0   100   200 km

Inset (Details)

D-DAY
June 6, 1944

Le Havre

Arromanches

Graye-sur-Mer

Courseulles

Bernières-sur-Mer

Orne R.

CAEN
July 1944

VERRIÈRES RIDGE
July 1944

Caen

Verrières

May-sur-Orne

Mezidon

CLOSING
THE FALAISE GAP
Aug 1944

Falaise

Trun

0   10   20 mi

0   10   20   30 km

CANVAS OF WAR

facing page:

Paul Goranson (1911–)

Posted to Newfie, 1942

Watercolour on art board

43.2 × 49.5 cm · CWM 11430

In December 1941, Paul Goranson enlisted in the Royal Canadian Air Force as a non-commissioned officer artist. Dispatched to Gander, Newfoundland, on temporary duty in February 1942, he completed dozens of sketches. "It was a different world—like outer space," he recalled. Later, he became an official war artist.

left:

Henry Lamb (1883–1960)

Portrait of Trooper Lloyd George Moore, (formerly entitled A *Redskin in the Canadian Royal Artillery*), 1942

Oil on canvas

76.2 × 63.5 cm · CWM 7833

Trooper Moore was a member of the Three Rivers Regiment. During the Second World War, 3090 Native Canadians enlisted, out of an estimated population of 126,000. There were more than 200 fatalities.

at the outset of the struggle. Many Canadians, watching with increasing disgust as Hitler rearmed Germany and overturned the 1919 peace settlement, viewed Canada's declaration of war in 1939 as nothing less than a moral duty. Others were interested in Europe—if at all— solely by way of cultural and family ties to the British Isles and viewed 1939 in terms not much different from 1914: Canada coming to the Mother Country's rescue once again in its hour of need. Many historians thereby argue that Canada, the only country in the Western Hemisphere to do so, went to war simply to support Britain. Unemployment was still very high and many Canadians enlisted simply to secure jobs and earn money after a decade of economic turmoil. Hundreds of thousands had little sympathy for the struggle at all, including many German, Italian and East European immigrants as well as members of Canada's vocal communist and socialist movements.

"What is striking about the first few days of the war," wrote historian J. L. Granatstein, "is the coolness of the Canadian response. There were the usual fire-eaters, of course, but they stand out only because they were so firmly in a minority."[2] Mackenzie King, reflecting on his government's earnest efforts to ensure domestic peace even as the country went to war, told Parliament that "Canada had come into the war with a quietude and peace almost comparable to that of a vessel sailing over a smooth and sunlit lake." Having "kept down all passion and faction," he observed with satisfaction, we "now were a united country."

Soldiers such as Howard Graham, an officer of the Hastings and Prince Edward Regiment and a First World War veteran, reflected on more mundane matters:

It is difficult to find words to express my feelings after I replaced the phone receiver that Friday afternoon of August 31, 1939. Colonel Young informed me that the regiment was being mobilized. When I had enlisted in 1916, it was with excitement and enthusiasm; the sense of adventure was in the air. I was leaving my family, but they [sic] were not dependent on me. I had no business to abandon. I was young and the future was mine. There were new countries to see, new friends to be made. Now, twenty-three years later, I was in my forty-second year and all was different. I hated the very thought of leaving my wife and son of six years and the home we had made and enjoyed together. Leaving a legal practice I had worked hard to develop and facing the thought of a substantial loss and going abroad now held no attraction for me.

What a fool I had been to spend time and money these past seventeen years on military affairs! Yet, I thought, I must be honest. I was only one of hundreds of Militia officers with families across Canada who would be feeling the same unhappy situation. We were not under any legal obligation to serve outside Canada until we signed an undertaking to do so. But to refuse to do that would have been in my opinion morally wrong and disloyal to the

T. R. MacDonald (1908–1978)

Night Travellers, c. 1943

Oil on canvas

51.1 × 81.5 cm · CWM 13177

One of the first war-related paintings official war artist T. R. MacDonald completed, this work is similar to his pre-war Canadian subjects and was one of his favourites. Later, he found himself in Italy faced with new challenges. In a 1977 interview, he commented: "All the sections of war brought up in illustrations of the Boer War and things like that of Russian troops and galloping cavalry; it wasn't like that at all, except the firing of guns sometimes. People kept under cover as much as possible. You didn't see people galloping around. All this was frightful, a real nightmare. I spent the night in trenches. But at that time I guess it was the second largest bombardment of the war somewhere up in the hills of Italy. This was to break down the German lines before the troops went in. But they would fire on anything you could imagine. They ringed field guns, all calibres, and surrounded them and we opened up after dark. The thunder and the flashes were just quite beyond anything I could have conceived."

E. J. Hughes (1913–)
Armoured Car, 1946
Oil on canvas
101.9 × 122.1 cm · CWM 12739

A service artist with the Canadian Army from November 1940 to January 1942, E. J. Hughes was appointed an official war artist on February 1, 1942, one of the very first. After a period with the First Special Service Force in the Aleutian Islands in 1943, he spent much of his time in southern England with the Royal Canadian Dragoons. He made dozens of sketches of armoured cars in preparation for this canvas.

left:

Moses Reinblatt (1917–1979)
Dismantling Bent Props, 1945
Oil on canvas
81.5 × 66.5 cm · CWM 11608

Recalling his fellow Royal Canadian Air Force official war artist "Moe" Reinblatt, Patrick Cowley-Brown wrote: "It seemed to me, [sic] that he possessed an independence of spirit, a self determination and a great excitement for painting. He was a civilized person and a good painter."

regiment and to the establishment that had trained me to carry out the duties I would now be required to perform. About these matters Jean [Graham's wife] agreed with me, though with sadness and reluctance. And so it was that I signed up for overseas service.[3]

Herb Peppard, later a member of the elite First Special Service Force, a Canadian-American brigade, described himself simply as a reluctant soldier who preferred to pile lumber in his native Truro, Nova Scotia, rather than go off to war. He relented in December 1940 after watching dozens of "those damned troop trains" pass through town on their way to Halifax.[4] Bob Loughlan from Thunder Bay, Ontario, was just sixteen in 1939 and could not wait to fight. "I could only dream and curse the fact that I was born two years too late. . . . I was certain that the war would be over before I would get my chance to show them all how a fight should be won."[5]

While Canada's first army contingent prepared to head overseas, its naval and air forces also swung into action. The navy quickly placed the important port of Halifax on a wartime footing, launching a large program to build coastal escort and minesweeping ships for the defence of Canada's territorial waters and to relieve ships of Britain's Royal Navy for service in Europe. Almost immediately, the Royal Canadian Navy's six modern destroyers began escorting merchant ships on the first twenty-four hours of their transatlantic passage to Europe, the first tentative forays for what would become, by 1945, the world's third-largest navy.

As in the First World War, Canada's open airspace, far from all likely combat zones, was ideal for training aircrew. The British Commonwealth Air Training Plan (BCATP) agreement, signed in December 1939 by Australia, Canada, Great Britain and New Zealand, saw Canada provide thousands of recruits, instructors and support personnel, and hundreds of millions of dollars, for a massive international project. In the first years of the war, dozens of airfields, schools and training facilities opened across Canada while many more existing airfields expanded. The influx of thousands of young men and women, many of them from overseas, exercised a profound social and economic effect on small Canadian towns such as Goderich, Ontario, and Yorkton, Saskatchewan. The BCATP also left a vast network of improved airfields that linked the country from coast to coast.

More important was the program's contribution to the Allied war effort. At its peak, the BCATP operated 107 schools and 184 ancillary units at 231 different sites across Canada from Charlottetown, Prince Edward Island, to Patricia Bay, British Columbia. By the time it ended on March 31, 1945, the plan had produced 131,553 pilots, navigators, bomb aimers, wireless operators, air gunners and flight engineers, including nearly 73,000 Canadians. United States President Franklin D. Roosevelt referred to Canada as the "Aerodrome of Democracy." Most of the Canadian BCATP graduates initially entered British squadrons, but part of the agreement called for the creation of separate Canadian units wherever feasible.

Louis Keene (1888–1972)
Nelson Wonders, 1940
Watercolour on paper
49.1 × 42.9 cm · CWM 14123

Although his paintings of the Siberian expedition of 1919 had been purchased by the Canadian War Memorials Fund, Louis Keene was, in both world wars, primarily a soldier. This painting of the London Blitz during the Second World War was purchased for the Canadian War Records collection.

A journalist's account in the London (England) *Evening Standard* of May 29, 1942, tells how one of Keene's paintings began the process of entering the collection of the Imperial War Museum: "I dropped in at the National Gallery to see the two new rooms of war pictures. . . . A good many of these works are by serving members of the Forces, some of whom have never exhibited before. A Canadian, Lieut-col. Keene, painted his own men practising putting out incendiary bombs. . . . Not long afterwards a major in the colonel's regiment visited the War Artists' Exhibition. 'My colonel could do better pictures than any of those on show here,' he told the authorities. It was suggested that the colonel should submit some of his work. His vivid incendiary bomb picture is included in the National Gallery show."

CANVAS OF WAR

facing page:

Rowley Murphy (1891–1975)
Seamen on Jetty Being Instructed on Bends and Hitches, 1943
Oil on panel
30.0 × 40.6 cm · CWM 10481

Working as an official war artist for the Royal Canadian Navy was not always the best of experiences, as Rowley Murphy found out when posted to Esquimalt, British Columbia: "I must admit that it is far from pleasant to be working in unsuitable, leaky buildings with *no heat* when outdoor temperatures are from 40 to 50 [°F]. The almost daily rain makes interior damp so great that water-colours are impossible to use if they are to have any crisp edges, . . . I should like to pay tribute to Commander Beament's [a fellow war artist] prediction of unexpected troubles ahead of me in which he was quite correct; as all he mentioned have materialized very unpleasantly, especially that of not being found in my 'office' from 9 to 5 P.M. like all good Naval Officers, when of course I was hard at work outdoors."

left:

Maurice Gagnon (1912–)
Remember Hong Kong!, n.d.
Ink on paper
91.0 × 59.5 cm · CWM 56-05-12-033

The fall of Hong Kong in December 1941 resulted in the death or wounding of 40 per cent of the 1975 Canadians sent to the island. A further 287 Canadians died in brutally harsh Japanese prisoner-of-war camps before the end of the war.

Patrick Cowley-Brown (1918–)
Air to Ground, 1945
Oil on canvas
61.3 × 81.3 cm · CWM 11078

Patrick Cowley-Brown enlisted in the
Royal Canadian Air Force in March 1941
and trained as a wireless air gunner. He
won the 1944 RCAF Art Competition in
which Peter Whyte came second, and
was subsequently appointed an official
war artist. His task was to depict the west
coast RCAF stations and the Canada-U.S.
Alaska Highway, a huge project undertaken to provide a land route for military
supply of the isolated American territory.

"I enjoyed almost total freedom of
movement. . . . The on-the-spot sketches
were done selectively and quickly. . . . On
my return to Ottawa, I would submit my
field sketches to the Air Historian. Sug-
gestions and recommendations were
made as to the development of certain
ones into easel paintings. . . . I followed
a regular daily routine in Ottawa. There
was not the sense of immediacy or
urgency to be found on the stations. I
worked in a much more relaxed manner;
had the time to reflect on my experiences
in the field and to feel my way comfort-
ably into the larger canvasses."

By 1942, Britain's Royal Air Force (RAF) slowly began to make good on its promise to consolidate the Canadians into distinctive RCAF squadrons, but the question of Canadianization remained a delicate, complicated, political and military issue for the rest of the war. Although a total of forty-seven RCAF squadrons were ultimately established overseas, over half of RCAF overseas aircrew served in British squadrons.

TOTAL WAR

While Canada's naval and air capabilities expanded during the winter of 1939–40 and Canada's army guarded British and Canadian coasts against possible invasion or commando attacks, German forces planned to follow up their lightning victory against Poland with an equally rapid assault on Western Europe. The next stage in Germany's blitzkrieg began in April and May with a series of swift, powerful and daring strokes against first Denmark and Norway, then Belgium, the Netherlands and France. Moving faster and farther than almost any Western defence experts had predicted, Nazi Germany achieved in three months what Germany's First World War armed forces had failed to accomplish in four years.

Led by its new panzer, or tank, divisions, and strongly supported by aircraft specially designed for ground attack, the German army defeated the combined Franco-British-Belgian-Dutch forces in a matter of weeks and drove the British Expeditionary Force into an epic and chaotic evacuation by sea from Dunkirk. Basil Bartlett, a captain in the British army, remembered hud-

dling along the beach with hundreds of strangers from other units, French and British, waiting to be evacuated: "During the night the Navy sent off its little boats. The sea was like glass. It was terribly exciting to hear sailors' voices and the splash of oars. Again and again the boats came in. And we duly loaded them up. It was queer to be loading up strange soldiers into strange boats and handing them over to strange sailors . . . we saved each other's lives. But we never saw each other's faces."[6] Most of the British army's heavy weapons, vehicles and armour had to be left behind. In June 1940, during the campaign's closing weeks, Britain sought to retrieve the situation by landing more troops, including a Canadian brigade, in France, but after a brief excursion amid gathering chaos, they returned quickly to England without having encountered German ground units.

The historic defeat astounded the world and left Canada as Britain's most important ally. If, as everyone wholly expected, Hitler followed up his success by invading Britain, the 1st Canadian Infantry Division, which had trained hard over the preceding winter, would be the only completely equipped and organized division in the British Isles available to meet the Germans. Canada sent a fighter squadron to Britain in May 1940, and it fought in the summer and fall against swarms of attacking German bombers in the Battle of Britain. Four destroyers from Canada's total of only seven (Britain had provided Canada with an additional destroyer in the fall of 1939) assisted in the evacuation from France and fought German submarines that attacked merchant shipping off Britain's shores. Canada did not have much military capacity in 1940, but what it did have was entirely committed in Britain's defence.

France's defeat, Italy's entry into the war on Germany's side in June 1940 and the threat to the British Isles softened Mackenzie King's desire to fight a "limited liability" war. Amid pointed complaints from Conservatives, veterans' organizations, provincial premiers and several federal cabinet ministers that Canada was not doing enough to help Britain in its hour of need, Ottawa authorized the mobilization of additional army divisions, expanded its naval building program and committed more financial resources to the war. The National Resources Mobilization Act (NRMA) made military duty compulsory for service in Canada, but not even the collapse of the Allied armies in France convinced the government to abandon its pledge that there would be no conscription for overseas service. NRMA troops, called "zombies" by those Canadians who deplored the men's refusal to enlist for general service overseas, soon became a focal point of social and political debate over the government's war effort. Government critics, racists and hotheads argued that the NRMA leaned too far towards protecting French Canada from the draft and not far enough towards doing Canada's bit to win the war.

Ottawa also entered the first of a series of bilateral agreements with Washington, moving considerably closer to the United States in the areas of defence planning, industrial production and economic policy. In

August 1940, the two countries established a Permanent Joint Board on Defence to prepare combined plans for North American defence. The United States, although still formally neutral, would go very far both to assist the British Commonwealth in the war against Hitler and to secure the Western Hemisphere. By mid-1941, both North American partners had deployed substantial forces to defend Newfoundland, which was strategically vital to protect transatlantic shipping routes, and were also co-operating in plans to defend the Pacific coast. St. John's, dubbed "Newfie John" by thousands of Allied sailors, would remain a favourite haunt for shore leave until the end of the war. Like the BCATP elsewhere in Canada, the combined Canadian-American military presence in Newfoundland would have a profound social and economic impact on the sparsely populated British colony.

Canadian warships based in St. John's, including many of the new corvettes built in Canadian shipyards, played a vital role in the war against Germany's powerful submarine, or U-boat, fleet. The corvettes, which were only sixty metres long and originally designed solely for coastal work, nevertheless carried an effective armament of depth charges (underwater explosives) and were the only warships available in adequate numbers to escort merchant ships across the Atlantic. The corvette crews, made up of young men who had little training and even less sea experience because of the desperate need to strengthen the anti-submarine forces as quickly as possible, suffered terribly in the treacherous seas between

Peter Whyte (1905–1966)

Control Tower, 1944

Oil on canvas

41.0 × 51.2 cm · CWM 14304

Artist Peter Whyte, a Royal Canadian Air Force photographer, was a second prize winner in the 1944 RCAF Art Competition.

In over forty small-scale paintings, he provided a detailed record of British Commonwealth Air Training Plan activities in Alberta.

Albert Cloutier (1902–1965)

Night Traffic, Gander,
Newfoundland, 1945
Oil on canvas
75.7 × 122.3 cm · CWM 11001

From 1941 to 1943, Albert Cloutier was
art director of the Wartime Information
Board in Ottawa, which was responsible
for providing Canadians with positive

information about the war. Subsequently
an official war artist with the Royal Canadian Air Force, he recalled the inspiration for this painting in a 1958 interview:
"I remember one night sitting in the
control tower of a station on the Canadian east coast watching [large numbers
of] bombers take off for the European
Theatre. Not only could I see them

take off but I could hear [the pilots']
voices—young, brash, frightened and
confident. Their voices told a story that
was an important part of what I was
seeing. That night I made sketches.
The painting was called *Night Traffic.*"

Paraskeva Clark (1898–1986)

Parachute Riggers, 1947
Oil on canvas
101.7 × 81.4 cm · CWM 14086

In December 1944, the National Gallery of Canada commissioned Paraskeva Clark to paint the activities of the Women's Division of the Royal Canadian Air Force. She expressed her difficult search for a dramatic subject matter in an August 1945 letter to director H. O. McCurry of the National Gallery: "After having some personal experience with life and activities of the Women's Divisions in the R.C.A.F. or Wrens [Women's Royal Canadian Naval Service], I lost all hope to see 'any drama' there. But I found exciting enough the fact that in some activities, women performed the jobs, previously done by men and thus, released (perhaps) some men for fighting duties or for war industries.

"You see, I feel that dramatic subject . . . is not among C.W.A.C. [Canadian Women's Army Corps] but among millions [of] women who stayed in their homes, carring [sic] on some jobs, some responsibilities plus their usual home duties,—with their hearts full of constant pain longing and sorrow for their men gone fighting. Being CWAC was the easiest thing to do, the most pleasant. Throwing off the eternal chores and drodgery [sic] of woman's life—woman entered a regulated orderly life, with one duty set upon each for so many hours each day, with the glory and glamour of uniform to top it! The jobs—mostly clerical, or as servants, cooks. All that is important, but where is drama?"

Newfoundland, Iceland and Northern Ireland. "Life aboard the corvettes was really awful," remembered Frank Curry, a young sailor. "They were always half under water, the mess decks would be covered with a foot of water with things floating around. I think most of us kept asking ourselves how nice boys like us ever ended up in such a horrible situation. We were the innocents just like all people caught up in war."[7]

Corvette captains and crews would learn by hard experience that dedication and bravery were poor substitutes for training, skill and high-technology equipment in defending merchant ships against German torpedo attack. In the first years of the war, despite some notable successes, the Royal Canadian Navy was sometimes stretched beyond its limits by enormous responsibilities as a result of the Allied navies' inability to counter the U-boat offensive. Both the sea and the Germans were unforgiving enemies. On April 30, 1943, however, the RCN's growing strength and effectiveness were reflected in the creation of Canadian Northwest Atlantic Command, an enormous area covering the sea approaches to Newfoundland and the Canadian east coast. Under Rear-Admiral L. W. Murray, it would be the only theatre of war commanded by a Canadian during the Second World War.

The Royal Air Force's Battle of Britain victory during the summer of 1940, in which a fighter squadron rushed from Canada and Canadian pilots in British squadrons participated, thwarted Hitler's invasion plans and helped deflect his attention. Seeking room for the Germanic peoples to expand in Eastern Europe, he broke his pact with the Soviet Union's Joseph Stalin and launched a massive surprise attack in June 1941. This, together with Japan's attack on U.S. and British forces in the Pacific on December 7, changed dramatically the character of the war. Hitler responded to Japan's attack by declaring war on the United States, thereby adding both of the world's most powerful states to his list of enemies in the space of just six months. In the short term, however, the string of Allied defeats continued unabated, with vast German gains in the Balkans, the Soviet Union and North Africa, and Japanese conquests in China, Southeast Asia and across the Pacific Ocean.

A Canadian air squadron and two battalions of troops played prominent if tragic parts in defending British colonies in the Far East. There was also a great expansion of the coastal defences in British Columbia, including warships and air squadrons that, in the harrowing subarctic conditions of the north Pacific, assisted the U.S. in the defence of Alaska. Later a full Canadian army brigade that included many home defence conscripts would join U.S. forces in reoccupying the island of Kiska in the Aleutian chain.

However, the main weight of Canada's effort continued, overwhelmingly, to be concentrated against Germany and Italy. Even greater in scale than the expansion of Canadian air and naval forces was the growth of the Canadian land forces in Britain. During the First World War, Canada had built up a large army corps of four divisions. By early 1943, Canada's

Donald C. Mackay (1906–1979)

Convoy, Afternoon, 1943

Oil on panel

30.0 × 40.6 cm · CWM 10400

In a 1978 interview, Donald C. Mackay commented on the importance of the war art program: "To some young artists it gave an opportunity to paint which they had never had before and which is unlikely they would have achieved within quite a number of years. Conditions in Canada were such that it was practically impossible to make a living as an artist unless you were a successful portrait painter. I can't think of more than a dozen artists who made a living from their other painting. In my time in the twenties and thirties, artists made money because they were teachers, illustrators, commercial artists, or engaged as consultants in some field or another, related to the arts, but they had very little time to carry on the act of producing paintings."

facing page:

Bruno Bobak (1923–)
Tank Convoy, 1944
Oil on canvas
76.2 × 101.6 cm · CWM 11992

Sapper Bruno Bobak had not yet met
his future wife, Private Molly Lamb,
when he won first prize at the 1944
Canadian Army Art Exhibition, and
she won second. Both were to become
official war artists shortly thereafter.

Working in their London, England,
studios and later in Ottawa, many of
the war artists used their field studies as
inspirations for finished compositions,
combining elements taken from several
sketches to create a single picture.
This painting combines imagery from
two works on paper. In one, the composition is virtually the same, but the
central vehicles depicted are armoured
cars. The Ram tanks are derived from
another study.

left:

Carl Schaefer (1903–1995)
Bomb Aimer, Battle of the Ruhr 1944, 1951
Watercolour and graphite on paper
107.9 × 69.5 cm · CWM 11786

No. 6 (Royal Canadian Air Force)
Group in Bomber Command lost 4272
officers and men in 41,000 sorties during
which its aircraft dropped 126,000 tons
of bombs, many in the industrial Ruhr
area of Germany. Official war artist
Carl Schaefer's energetic but focussed
brush strokes capture the tension of the
moment when a bomb aimer signals the
release of the aircraft's bomb load.

land forces overseas constituted a full field army, First Canadian Army, that included I and II Canadian Corps, with five full divisions—three infantry and two armoured, that is, equipped with tanks. There were also two additional tank brigades to give increased striking power, and a vast array of communications, mechanical repair and other logistical units required to sustain such a force in fast-paced mechanized warfare. The growing size of Canada's military entailed far greater efforts on the home front as well. Producing the food, weapons and supplies necessary to keep Canada's troops in the field and to assist struggling allies such as Britain and, after June 1941, Russia, made unprecedented demands on government, business and labour.

Women overcame social custom and gender discrimination by entering industrial and agricultural production by the tens of thousands and, after July 1941, by enlisting in the Women's Auxiliary Air Force (later the Royal Canadian Air Force (Women's Division), or WD) and the Canadian Women's Army Corps (CWAC). After July 1942, they joined the Women's Royal Canadian Naval Service (WRCNS) as well, performing vital non-combat functions such as analysis of secret intelligence and air traffic control, extending far beyond traditional clerical duties. By war's end, nearly fifty thousand women had worked as nurses, some just behind the front lines in Italy and Northwest Europe, operated naval supply and communications facilities and air traffic control centres from British Columbia to the British Isles and carried out essential administrative

duties for all three armed forces. Their service and their sacrifice helped advance women's rights, but women fought social forces ranging from polite scepticism over their military utility to federal legislation that denied them equal pay and benefits. Especially during the early part of the war, a hurtful whispering campaign also accused women in uniform of low morals and bad character, laying at their feet responsibility for everything from venereal disease to family breakdowns.

A Jesuit priest, whose views were read into the House of Commons debates by a sympathetic member of Parliament, foresaw fewer marriages as young women, their health ruined by work in munition factories, proved unable to find mates. "After six months of slow poisoning," he noted, "she is debilitated, sallow-complexioned, exhausted, underweight, uncurable [sic], and she has not one cent for medical treatment . . . her suitor no longer sees her, offended by her new manners that are too vulgar."[8] A coordinated effort after the war to have women workers and military personnel return to home, family and traditional jobs was a sad end to their wartime efforts. In many areas, however, including access to veterans' benefits and society's acceptance of married women working outside the home, women secured a degree of equality and self-confidence undreamed of in the pre-war period. "It was the first time I was an individual and treated as one,"[9] recalled Aircraftwoman, Second Class, Shirley Smith, who worked at a BCATP flying school in Brantford, Ontario.

Harold Beament (1898–1984)

Burial at Sea, 1944

Oil on canvas

60.5 × 76.0 cm · CWM 10005

Harold Beament describes the event:
"We were in [an] attack in the Gulf of St.
Lawrence, and the [*Inger Elisabeth*] was
torpedoed, and one of the merchant service fellows on the bridge was blown off
the bridge into the sea. And I dispatched
a boat, had him picked up, but he was
dead . . . so I decided to get rid of the
body. I conducted a service at sea, which
was very tricky because we weren't sure
just what submarine strength there was
around us. . . . And so I decided to give
the chap a decent send off and I did it in
that way with the correct thing. The only
thing I didn't like doing, but I thought,
what the hell, was stopping engines as
the body went over the side—part of the
ceremony. And then full speed ahead
as fast as you can go because you didn't
want the Jerries [Germans] to get a sight
on you and run the torpedo while you
were sitting like a duck. So the thing
was memorable to me."

facing page:

Tom Wood (1913–1997)
The Boarding of the U-744, 1944
Oil on canvas
76.5 × 102.0 cm · CWM 10545

U-744 was destroyed by the Canadian support group C-2 on March 6, 1944, with HMCS *Chilliwack* putting a boarding party on the sinking wreck in an effort to recover radio code books and equipment.

In a 1979 interview, Tom Wood, an official war artist attached to the Royal Canadian Navy, described his experience: "It was a job. You felt good because you had a job and were able to paint. At the back of your mind was the Depression. The war broadened horizons, but for the most part, war is boring. There are long periods of inactivity and when there is action, it tends to be abrupt, impersonal and to some extent, abstract."

left:

E. J. Hughes (1913–)
Patrol, Kiska, 1945
Oil on canvas
76.0 × 91.2 cm · CWM 12962

The 13th Canadian Infantry Brigade attacked the island of Kiska in the Aleutian chain on August 15, 1943, as part of a U.S.-led invasion, only to find the Japanese had withdrawn on July 28. E. J. Hughes was the only Canadian artist to depict this event.

Women were not the only ones to face social hurdles and overt discrimination during the war. As in the First World War, "enemy aliens," or Canadians of German, Italian and Japanese descent, attracted suspicion from the authorities and from their neighbours because of their heritage and imagined political affiliations. Popular fears that spies hiding within the local community might disrupt defence plans, as they had elsewhere in the Pacific, led to demands that all potential saboteurs, especially Japanese Canadians living on Canada's west coast, be detained for the duration of hostilities. There were fascists and militarists within each "enemy alien" community as well as former soldiers and some enemy reservists, but there was little evidence of an imminent security threat. In the Japanese case, Allied defeats in the Pacific in 1941–42 and the long reach of the Japanese Imperial Navy seemed to pose a real military threat to British Columbia, many of whose residents, in part for economic reasons, were only too willing to remove local Japanese Canadians from their communities.

Prejudice, competitiveness, greed and military necessity thus combined, in one of the more infamous incidents in modern Canadian history, to relocate thousands of Japanese Canadians from British Columbia to centres elsewhere in Canada. The argument, that the move was made in part to protect them from local retribution, carried little weight with families whose possessions and property local authorities soon confiscated. Although there was a real danger from hooligans,

just as there may have been a limited security threat, removing Japanese Canadians (and arresting and interning many other Canadians suspected of disloyalty) was due to far more complex causes. Canadians acted in many cases with the best interests of their country at heart—it was, after all, a time of war—but they also acted in part from fear, paranoia and racism.

The fate of one Canadian army contingent in the Pacific at the hands of Japanese troops did little to calm Canadian passions. Sent to Hong Kong in late 1941 to help deter Japanese aggression, nearly two thousand Canadian troops fell victim to an overwhelming attack as Tokyo's forces swept across the entire region beginning on December 7, 1941. Despite ferocious resistance and some eight hundred casualties, the Canadians, along with the rest of the garrison, surrendered on Christmas Day amid an orgy of rape, murder and torture by the victorious Japanese troops. Kay Christie, a nursing sister at the British Military Hospital in Kowloon, recalled the surrender. After killing many of the patients, Japanese troops "went after the nursing sisters and volunteers. They stripped them, they slapped their faces with their Red Cross arm bands and started raping them on top of the mattresses that had the corpses underneath. This went on and on. Then for some reason . . . they took three of the volunteers and, after raping them, cut their heads off and piled their naked bodies outside."[10] The survivors sat out the rest of the war in Japanese prisoner-of-war camps under barbaric conditions, blatantly illegal under international law. Underfed, overworked

Jack Shadbolt (1909–1998)
Incoming and Outgoing Guards, 1944
Watercolour on paper
53.3 × 75.6 cm · CWM 14265

Excerpt from war diary, internment camp at Petawawa, Ontario: "23 Oct 44 2/Lieut [Jack] Shadbolt an Army Artist arrived this afternoon and is expected to remain two or three weeks to do some painting of Internment Camp scenes for Historical Section N.D.H.Q." Members of the Veterans Guard of Canada were responsible for the camp's security.

CANVAS OF WAR

facing page:

Harold Beament (1898–1984)

Passing?, c. 1944

Oil on canvas

61.1 × 76.5 cm · CWM 10055

An official war artist attached to the Royal Canadian Navy, Harold Beament had seen service in the First World War. As he said in a 1979 interview: "A lot of the time . . . it was kind of difficult to separate the Naval Officer from the War Artist in thinking and resolving just how I would tackle certain problems. For example I used to work a lot at night in my studio in London . . . and I'd be very pleased with the canvas when I went to bed. I'd wake up in the morning and of course the canvas was right in front of me and I'd think, good God, I wouldn't put to sea in that vessel if that was the last thing I did. It's not seaworthy and I'd start making it seaworthy from the naval officer's point of view."

left:

Robert Hyndman (1915–)

Flight Lieutenant C. F. Schaefer, c. 1945

Oil on canvas

76.0 × 55.7 cm · CWM 11569

Official war artist Robert Hyndman said of this painting: "I was very happy doing it . . . nobody told me to do it. I found it was just happening as a painting for instance in his hand, which was fun to paint and this other hand, the cap, the relationship. And this is the sort of stormy sky he would paint. I think that's about the best painting I did in the war. That is Carl [war artist Carl Schaefer] as I knew him."

Goodridge Roberts (1904–1974)

Canadian Airmen in a Park, 1944
Watercolour on paper
43.5 × 59.9 cm · CWM 11670

Goodridge Roberts, of the Royal
Canadian Air Force, worried about the
role of the official war artist. In a 1943
letter to H. O. McCurry, director of the
National Gallery, he wrote: "In a sense
the fact that the work is to be primarily
a record makes the responsibility of

the artist greater than if he were to be
producing pictures for immediate propaganda use. For in the one case real artistic worth is a requisite, while in the other
a certain aptness and honest workman-
ship would be enough."

He seems never to have been satis-
fied with his own work, and like other
war artists felt the weather was unhelpful.
In February 1944, he wrote to McCurry:
"Unfortunately my output so far has been

both small and unimportant. In order
to do some painting that I can really feel
some satisfaction with I long above all for
some summer weather. Without trying to
pass the buck, I lay most of the blame for
my meagre output to date at the feet of
the winds. With a damp cold wind tearing over the countryside my mind tends
to turn to thoughts of a cup of tea an [sic]
a spot of shelter." Good weather, perhaps,
produced this painting.

and regularly abused, some 287 Canadians died in the camps while hundreds more returned crippled, maimed and emotionally scarred.

While Allied forces reeled from successive Japanese attacks in the Pacific in 1942, Allied naval forces in the Atlantic were very hard pressed by Germany's effective submarine offensive. U-boats roaming the Gulf of St. Lawrence, well into the mouth of the St. Lawrence River, sank over twenty merchant ships and several Canadian warships, some of them within sight of shore. At Bell Island, Newfoundland, U-boats on two occasions in the fall of 1942 penetrated into a narrow channel between the mainland and the small island's docking facilities to sink a total of four merchant ships loading iron ore. On the coast of Labrador, the Germans established an automatic weather station to transmit data vital to forecasting conditions on the combat fronts in Europe. Less effective was their landing of spies, one on the Quebec shore of Baie des Chaleurs, who was immediately apprehended by provincial police, and a second on the New Brunswick shore of Bay of Fundy, who later surrendered to the Royal Canadian Mounted Police. Canadian aircraft, fitted to drop explosive charges that would detonate underwater, soon drove the U-boats out of coastal waters, but at mid-Atlantic, beyond the range of Allied land-based aircraft, the enemy submarines were then able to mass against merchant ship convoys and inflict crippling losses.

The Allies would not have been able to counter effectively the mid-Atlantic attacks without over one hundred Canadian corvettes and destroyers that held the line while Britain's Royal Navy created special anti-submarine hunting forces. These hunting forces, with help from Canadian warships that were beginning to receive better weapons and training, drove back the U-boats from the main shipping lanes in May 1943. At the same time, RCAF maritime squadrons, based in Newfoundland, Nova Scotia and the British Isles, received longer-range aircraft to strengthen the defences at mid-ocean. Later in the war, new snorkel breathing devices allowed the U-boats to stay under water for greater periods and once again carry the war close to British and Canadian shores, but the RCN and the RCAF proved equal to the challenge. Canadian warships and aircraft sank, or shared in the sinking of, fifty U-boats during the war, twenty-eight of them in 1944–45, but lost many of their number in return. On April 16, 1945, three weeks before Germany's surrender, a U-boat sank the minesweeper HMCS *Esquimalt*, the last Canadian warship lost during the war, within sight of Halifax.

In the air, the BCATP ensured that Canadians were overrepresented in the Royal Air Force and at first most served in British, not Canadian, squadrons. The formation on January 1, 1943, of No. 6 (Royal Canadian Air Force) Group in Bomber Command helped correct this imbalance but RCAF squadrons suffered enormous losses in their first missions. At one point, the chance of a Canadian flier surviving his thirty-mission tour was just one in ten. "We didn't realize, nobody realized, the casualties," recalled Alan MacLeod, an air navigator, but

Charles Comfort (1900–1994)
Dieppe Raid, 1946
Oil on canvas
91.4 × 152.7 cm · CWM 12276

The disastrous Dieppe Raid of August 19, 1942, resulted in 70 per cent of the 4963 Canadians who participated being killed, wounded or taken prisoner. Charles Comfort reconstructed the event from written records, personal recollections and photographs.

right:

Lawren P. Harris (1910–1994)

Private W. A. Haggard, c. 1942

Oil on canvas

55.9 × 45.9 cm · CWM 12691

Private Haggard, a member of the South Saskatchewan Regiment, was awarded the Distinguished Conduct Medal for his actions during the ill-fated Dieppe landing in August 1942. Lawren P. Harris painted a number of portraits of Dieppe survivors.

facing page:

Lawren P. Harris (1910–1994)

Reinforcements Moving up in the Ortona Salient, 1946

Oil on canvas

76.3 × 102.1 cm · CWM 12712

One of the first official war artists hired, Lawren P. Harris served with the Armoured Corps, and he considered this his most successful painting.

In a 1979 interview, he talked about his working methods: "To sit down and actually draw a tank would take you a dickens of a time, with all the tracks and the bogies and so on. I took a lot of pictures and sometimes when nothing was going on would actually sit down and draw one just to get the feel of the thing. The sketches that I did on the spot didn't have all that great detail but at any time you wanted to work the canvas, you had the detail in your sketches or in your photographs."

"a lot of guys don't come back and you never know which one it's going to be."[11] Canadian aviators, like their naval brothers-in-arms on the North Atlantic, learned from bitter experience that training, skill and technical proficiency were essential to survive, in addition to a generous amount of luck. No. 6 Group and the fifteen squadrons of Canadian fighter aircraft in No. 83 Group of the RAF's Second Tactical Air Force formed the core of Canada's forty-seven-squadron commitment overseas. Even with these large Canadian formations, however, over 50 per cent of the RCAF's overseas air-crew served in RAF squadrons. Overall, 232,632 men and 17,030 women served in the RCAF during the war, 17,101 of whom lost their lives.

THE LONG ROAD BACK

Although Canada's growing army overseas prepared incessantly for eventual combat, for a long time most Canadian troops remained out of the fight, in the British Isles. Like hundreds of thousands of other Allied troops, they waited for the decision to attack Hitler's Europe with a mixture of disappointment and gratitude. Few wanted recklessly to lead the attack on German-occupied France, but the long months spent in England strained Canadian discipline (and British patience) in familiar ways. In the First World War, Canadians had earned a reputation as effective, even brilliant, fighting troops, but they were also considered an occasionally undisciplined and insubordinate lot whose time in England was frequently punctuated by run-ins with

local authority and reprimands from their officers. The Canadians were not the only colonials so censured, but a series of demobilization riots in 1918–19 appeared to confirm the impression that Canadians, although unbeatable at the front, were also intolerable behind it.

In the early days of the the Second World War, especially during the first winters, Canada's new army in Britain appeared ready to adopt its predecessor's mantra. As historians C. P. Stacey and Barbara M. Wilson point out, part of the problem was simply that the 1st Division had received little military training before its arrival. Bad weather, poor—and often unheated—accommodation combined with Britain's far more permissive drinking laws to shape the relationship between Canada's home-sick citizen-soldiers and the British public. "Fog and rain," recorded Paul M. Irwin of the Royal Canadian Ordnance Corps morosely in his diary. "How lousy this English weather can be. . . . I read an old quotation in *The Daily Mirror* today, 'He also serves who only stands and waits.' Whoever he was and when, he was perhaps thinking of the 1940–41 version of the Canadian Army."

After censoring Canadian army mail, British authorities reported on the widespread dissatisfaction of Canadian troops:

- Boredom, homesickness and a feeling of not being really needed appear to be the major reasons why nearly all these Canadian soldiers grumble. The majority of the writers warn their friends and relatives not to join the army.

Tony Law (1916–1996)
Canadian Tribal Destroyers in Action, 1946
Oil on canvas
102.2 × 153.0 cm · CWM 10248

The Royal Canadian Navy acquired its four powerful Tribal-class destroyers, *Athabaskan*, *Haida*, *Huron* and *Iroquois*, in 1942–43. Shown here is one of the many intense night actions fought with German warships in the English Channel. Tony Law, a serving naval officer and an official war artist, commanded a motor-torpedo boat flotilla. In an interview, Law commented: "They had quite a battle that night with the German destroyers. They drove one up on the rocks. . . . It's very hard to paint night actions . . . star shells coming down . . . you felt naked when they put them up over you in a torpedo boat."

facing page:

Will Ogilvie (1901–1989)

Tanks Moving into Dittaino Valley
Sicily, 1943
Watercolour and graphite on paper
57.3 × 78.4 cm · CWM 13618

Will Ogilvie was the only war artist present during the invasion of Sicily in July 1943. His February 1944 report provides a detailed, idiosyncratic, if somewhat detached, account of preparations. "A small book *Italy* was issued to all ranks. This compact booklet had an excellent foreword and contained much useful information. What seemed to be particularly valuable was a very brief history of Italy and an explanation of Italian customs and character. It was stressed also that Italy was a storehouse of cultural and historic monuments which should be respected by all as being a legacy. In a practical way, the book dealt with simple phrases in Italian which the soldier might need in asking directions, giving instructions to civilians, requesting certain types of food, etc."

left:

Austin Taylor (1908–1992)

Off-Hours, 1945
Egg tempera on cardboard
77.0 × 60.0 cm · CWM 19930074-001

Sapper Austin Taylor won first prize with this painting at the 1945 Canadian Army Art Exhibition. Servicemen were encouraged to paint and draw through organized art and exhibit programs, in part to fend off boredom and low morale in the long periods of inaction that characterized much of military life.

- The recent bad weather has made them dislike this country considerably. . . .
- The insufficiency and bad quality of the food annoys the majority of the writers.[12]

Throughout the war, Canadian and British authorities sought to maintain good relations between civilians and military personnel. On the Canadian side, carefully organized athletic competitions, hobbies, educational courses and cultural visits tried to ease the burden of ceaseless training and the boredom caused by long months of inaction. "The inactivity gets the boys," Paul Irwin confided to his diary. "The following sign in one of the Inf. Unit's mess: 'Never has so little been done by so many for so long.'" General McNaughton believed that educational training would benefit his troops overseas and began planning courses while he was en route to England. Meeting civilians, during billets and meals at private homes, social events and dates, helped many Canadians settle into their new surroundings, but drunkenness and rowdy behaviour caused intermittent problems throughout the war. Letters of complaint reached all the way to the desk of Canada's prime minister. Letters and packages from home boosted morale for personnel overseas far better, but sports and recreation programs, from knitting competitions to intramural softball and hockey, occupied idle hours too. When the European war ended in 1945, a khaki university opened to prepare the troops for their return to "civvy street" (the civilian world).

The troops' grumbling about Britain's poor food and bad weather worried Canadian commanders, but such complaints echoed the age-old grousing of soldiers deployed far from home. Napoleon Bonaparte, a century and a half earlier, had called his own impressive army *les grognards*, or old grumblers. Did the Canadians' complaints reflect deeper problems with morale and commitment? Early press accounts of Canada's greatest military fiasco of the war, the Dieppe Raid in August 1942, later cited by many historians, noted that the Canadians, bored, ready and spoiling for a fight, had somehow pressured the high command into action.

Denis Whitaker, a veteran of the battle, dismisses such assertions as sheer myth, the direct result of official propaganda attempting to cover up a colossal strategic mistake. "We weren't 'browned off,'" Whitaker, an officer in the Royal Hamilton Light Infantry, remembered. Nor did the men think they were languishing in England, as some accounts claimed. "If we'd been ordered to battle, anywhere, we would have gone, with determination and enthusiasm—as we did, to Dieppe. After all, we had volunteered to fight and we respected that commitment. But we certainly weren't agitating for it. . . . I sure wasn't pushing my neck out and saying I wanted to get shot at."[13] Canada's generals, minister of national defence and government wanted the raid to appease various political forces at home and abroad, Whitaker argued, and the soldiers had little choice but to comply.

Whitaker and his companions might have preferred anywhere other than where they were sent. On August

Will Ogilvie (1901–1989)
*Horsa Gliders of the 6th Airborne
Division, 1944,* c. 1946
Oil on canvas
53.3 × 81.5 cm · CWM 13394

The gliders have crashed at the mouth
of the Orne River, in Normandy, to the
east of the Canadian landing beaches.

COMFORT 48

facing page:

Charles Comfort (1900–1994)
The Hitler Line, 1944
Oil on canvas
101.6 × 121.7 cm · CWM 12296

From Charles Comfort's diary: "One gun created a fantastic sight, sticking perpendicularly up into the air, like a gigantic pylon memorializing the disasters of war. A direct hit had detonated its magazine, the resulting blast tearing the whole turret from its casemate and tossing it in the air. There it was, a vast, inert steel probe, blindly challenging the heavens."

left:

Charles Comfort (1900–1994)
Major W. A. Ogilvie, 1948
Watercolour on paper
83.8 × 78.7 cm · CWM 4978

Will Ogilvie was a Canadian Army service artist from October 1940 and, after the war art program was launched, an official war artist until September 1946. He painted in Britain, Italy and Northwest Europe.

THE CANADIAN ARMY
IN SICILY AND ITALY
1943–45

Route of
Canadian Army
Canadian battles   ORTONA
                          Dec 1943
National boundaries of 1939

Milan

Trieste

Fiume

Venice

Turin

BATTLE OF THE RIVERS
Dec 1944

Ravenna

Ligurian

Sea

Gothic
Line

BREAKING
THE GOTHIC LINE
Aug–Sept 1944

Rimini

Florence

Livorno

YUGOSLAVIA

Adriatic Sea

CORSICA
(France)

ORTONA
Dec 1943

Pescara

Ortona

MORO RIVER
Nov–Dec 1943

Moro R.

Petacciato

Rome

Casacalenda
Campobasso

Hitler
Line

Cassino

BREAKING
THE HITLER LINE
May 1944

Naples

Potenza

Taranto

Tyrrhenian

SARDINIA

Sea

*Gulf of
Taranto*

Ionian

Sea

N

CROSSING THE
STRAITS OF MESSINA
Sept 1943

Reggio di
Calabria

Messina

Palermo

M
e
d
i
t
e
r
r
a
n
e
a
n

0   50   100   mi
0   100   200   km

Agira

Dittaino R.

Catania

SICILY

LANDINGS IN SICILY
July 10, 1943

Pachino

S   e   a

TUNISIA

19, 1942, after months of Russian pressure on London and Washington to open a second front against Germany somewhere on the European continent to ease the pressure on the Soviet Red Army, the Western Allies launched a major raid on the French port of Dieppe. Five thousand of the six thousand men who participated in the attack were drawn from the 2nd Canadian Infantry Division. Most of the remainder were British commandos. The purpose of the raid was to test Germany's coastal defences and keep as many troops as possible from being sent to reinforce the Russian front. Everything went wrong. "She was rough, boy, she was sure rough," recalled one Canadian survivor. "It was like all hell had split open, the racket, my God, boy, the racket, the shells and the holy uproar."[14] The small seaside town, located on the English Channel between some of the most forbidding cliffs in Western Europe, was well defended by German infantry and artillery. The attacking Canadian force struck shortly after dawn, without tactical surprise, and without adequate naval and air support. The result was a slaughter. Whitaker remembers seeing "the beaches of hell" when he landed with the Royal Hamilton Light Infantry. "The ramp dropped. I led the thirty odd men of my platoon in a charge about twenty-five yards up the stony beach. We fanned out and flopped down just short of a huge wire obstacle. Bullets flew everywhere. Enemy mortar bombs started to crash down. Around me, men were being hit and bodies were piling up, one on top of the other. It was terrifying."[15]

John Williamson, also in Whitaker's unit, struggled through the surf towards shore. "Tracer started coming at us even before we got to shore. We said, what the hell goes on? This wasn't supposed to happen. Then I was hit. Soon there was only one man left in our platoon who was not killed or wounded." A German veteran praised the Canadians' bravery. "Nobody thought of giving up. Taking effective cover behind their dead comrades, they [the Canadians] shot uninterruptedly at our positions. Thus with their bodies these dead soldiers provided their comrades with the last service of friendship."[16] The raiders lost 3367 casualties, including 907 dead and 1946 captured. It was Canada's greatest defeat of the war.

In 1943, the Western Allies returned to Europe, first invading Sicily in July 1943, then the Italian mainland in September. German troops fought skilfully for every mountaintop and road junction as they retreated across Sicily's rugged terrain. Canadians joined Britain's Eighth Army for the invasion, but not without controversy. Under pressure at home for its failure to use Canada's large army anywhere other than Hong Kong and Dieppe, Ottawa arranged for the 1st Canadian Infantry Division (in England since December 1939) and the 1st Canadian Army Tank Brigade to participate in the attack, despite General McNaughton's objections. Remembering the successful experience of the Canadian Corps in 1915–18, McNaughton wanted to keep the Canadians together to participate in the eventual campaign to invade Western Europe and advance on

CANVAS OF WAR

facing page:

Orville Fisher (1911–1999)
D-Day—the Assault, 1945
Oil on canvas
102.1 × 122.6 cm · CWM 12469

In a 1964 interview, Orville Fisher described landing in France on D-Day: "The noise was unbearable, even off-shore. The big battle wagons, cruisers, destroyers and rocket ships were all throwing shells at the coast. The din was terrific. The coast was a neutral land-scape—greys and khaki and dark browns when the khaki uniforms got wet. The only bright colors on the beach were the flags showing where each unit was to land. . . . The water was literally red with blood. It ebbed and flowed with the tide. . . . I had a three-inch square water-color pack and a hand-sized sketch pad—with waterproof paper—that had a strap fitted over my palm. I used glycerin with water colors to make a fast series of sketches—like shorthand notes."

left:

Eric Aldwinckle (1909–1980)
Invasion Pattern Normandy, c. 1945
Oil on canvas
85.6 × 85.7 cm · CWM 10679

Graye-sur-Mer shortly after D-Day. The title of the painting draws attention to the identification markings on the wings of the Mustang, distinctive to the Allied aircraft committed to the Normandy assault, and to the pattern of activity on the ground below.

Germany itself. By the end of the year, McNaughton's objections to Canada's growing commitments in the Mediterranean led to his replacement by Lieutenant-General H. D. G. Crerar.

The 1st Division suffered more than twenty-three hundred casualties in Sicily, the fighting's ferocity providing a foretaste of the greater campaign soon to follow on the mainland. At Ortona, a small town on Italy's Adriatic coast, the Canadians spent Christmas battling house to house against elite German paratroopers, capturing the town but with more than 650 killed and wounded in the eight-day battle. Strome Galloway spent Christmas Day under constant machine-gun fire, coordinating an attack by The Royal Canadian Regiment. "Outside our building men were dying," he recalled. "In the muddy vineyards they found their peace on earth—the Christmas message through the ages. But they didn't hear any angels sing, only the stutter of machine guns, the crack of rifles and the screaming, whining and thudding of shells and mortar bombs. They were as far from Bethlehem as Man could ever get."[17]

After the Allied invasion of France in June 1944, troops committed to the Italian campaign were often overlooked in the newsreels and propaganda reports of the war effort and, all too frequently, in later histories of the war. The Italian campaign was smaller and less strategically important than the battles in France or Russia, but the "D-Day Dodgers," to quote a contemporary description of Commonwealth troops in Italy, fought a long, bitter campaign against some of Ger-

many's finest troops. By the winter of 1943–44, Canada's contribution had grown into I Canadian Corps, with the arrival of an armoured division and support troops. From the spring of 1944 until February–March 1945 when they transferred to Northwest Europe, the Canadians in Italy built a reputation as a highly effective, hard-hitting formation. In May 1944, the Canadians helped crack the so-called Hitler Line of German defences south of Rome; in an even more successful operation in August–September, they broke through the heavily defended Gothic Line, the Germans' main system of fortifications in northern Italy. Such successes came at a steep price: of the 93,000 Canadians who served in Italy, 5764 died and 20,000 were wounded.

When the Allies returned to France on D-Day, June 6, 1944, thousands of Canadians participated in the assault. At sea, more than one hundred Canadian warships protected the invasion force, carried troops and bombarded the German-occupied coast; from the air, hundreds of Canadian aircraft bombed roads, bridges and railways, attacked coastal defences and protected the invasion area from enemy aircraft. Inland, Allied paratroopers, including the 1st Canadian Parachute Battalion, landed to seize key bridges and towns behind the invasion beaches. On the ground, the Allied supreme command assigned one of the five invasion beaches to the 3rd Canadian Infantry Division and 2nd Canadian Armoured Brigade. "Everyone seemed calm and ready," Company Sergeant-Major Charles Martin, "A" Company, the Queen's Own

Orville Fisher (1911–1999)
Battle for Carpiquet Airfield, 1946
Oil and graphite on canvas
102.0 × 122.0 cm · CWM 12421

Despite a determined and costly attack by the 8th Canadian Infantry Brigade on July 4, 1944, Carpiquet airfield remained in German hands until Caen was taken on July 9, 1944. Orville Fisher used the image of a destroyed but still standing aircraft hangar to symbolize this determined and ultimately successful action.

George Pepper (1903–1962)

Tanks Moving up for the Breakthrough, 1946

Oil on canvas

81.2 × 122.0 cm · CWM 13795

Official war artist George Pepper went missing for a period, as related by a newspaper account: "Late in 1944 while he [Pepper] and another officer were en route to a liberated town, they met a German soldier standing erect in a slit trench. They captured him without difficulty, but when they were transferring him to the jeep he turned on them and tried to take away the rifle. The other officer shot the prisoner dead. But the sound of the shot roused other enemy soldiers and the two Canadians themselves were forced to hole up in the trench. His friend was shot and Capt. Pepper hid for ten days in the trench, his escape cut off, and only ditch water to drink. Finally he did manage to escape and was picked up by a British patrol."

Rifles of Canada, remembered, as his assault boat filled with men approached the beach at Bernières-sur-Mer. "The order rang out: 'Down ramp.' The moment the ramp came down, heavy machine-gun fire broke out from somewhere back of the seawall. Mortars were dropping all over the beach." Martin and his men raced forward. Many fell, but the beach was captured.[18]

After landing successfully, Canadian troops supported by tanks, naval gunfire and fighter bombers of Second Tactical Air Force, (RAF), which included a large number of Canadian squadrons, pushed through the German coastal defences and rushed inland to enlarge the bridgehead. The Germans were in no mood to give ground. Allied deception measures had convinced Hitler that the Normandy landings were a feint to draw attention away from the main landing area farther to the northeast, but German forces nevertheless reacted quickly to the invasion, moving tanks and infantry into the invaders' path. The Allies' push inland stalled just kilometres from the coast. Canadian and British formations, facing more German armour and mechanized units than their American counterparts, fought ferociously through the rest of June, July and much of August, first for the vital city of Caen and then to push southward towards the ancient town of Falaise, the strategic key to the whole of northwestern France and the route to Paris. At Carpiquet airfield near Caen, well-hidden German 88-millimetre anti-tank guns destroyed dozens of Canadian tanks in a desperate struggle. "Everywhere men lay dead or dying," recalled an army chaplain.[19]

After hard fighting, American troops, who had landed farther west along the Normandy coast, broke through the German positions late in July and began moving inland. British, Canadian and Polish forces, literally having to blast their way, kilometre by kilometre, through the strong German defences, tried to link up with the Americans, now advancing in a broad sweep from the southwest, in an attempt to encircle several hundred thousand German troops now fleeing eastward to escape the trap. It was far easier said than done. Charlie Martin remembered the incredible destruction that marked the German army's fighting retreat to Falaise. At Maizières, the sunken roads "were littered every foot of the way with corpses and burned equipment. The stench made us sick."[20] Several well-planned attacks failed to crack the German lines, despite considerable ingenuity by Canadian commanders and incredible bravery by the troops. Some tragic mistakes resulted in slaughter, such as an unsupported attack in broad daylight against Verrières Ridge by Montreal's Black Watch regiment, but Canadian troops acquitted themselves well against ferocious German resistance.

As Allied forces pushed south and east to encircle German forces in a pincer movement, the fighting all along the Canadian front was close, desperate and bloody. Aware of the danger, the well-trained German formations, although outnumbered and almost completely without air cover, resisted savagely to escape the narrowing gap near Falaise; Canadian and Polish troops attacked with equal determination to close it.

facing page:

Michael Forster (1907–)

Vestiges of Mulberry, Arromanches, 1945
Gouache and crayon on light brown paper
70.7 × 94.9 cm · CWM 10229

An official war artist with the Royal Canadian Navy, Michael Forster painted scenes of naval activity in the English Channel. The artificial Mulberry Harbour off Arromanches, France, was the key to supplying the invading Allied forces after June 6, 1944.

left:

Robert Hyndman (1915–)

Dive Bombing v-1 Sites, France, 1945
Oil on canvas
76.5 × 102.1 cm · CWM 11532

Robert Hyndman was an experienced Spitfire pilot with the Royal Canadian Air Force as well as a war artist. In his words: "We would go down, straight down from 14,000 with the 500-pound bomb there, and you'd release . . . and pull out and get the hell home. And he [fellow airman Squadron Leader N. R. Fowlow] didn't make it, he was hit on the way down, he just blew up in a million pieces. It's funny, we went back to the squadron and everybody was deathly silent, you know nobody said a word and suddenly one fellow said 'Well . . . he got his ears squashed that time didn't he.'"

Caven Atkins (1907–)

Forming Bulkhead Girders, 1942
Watercolour on paper
58.6 × 80.1 cm · CWM 14057

The National Gallery acquired a number of watercolours by Caven Atkins completed at the Toronto Shipbuilding Company. "I would like to make a comment on one of my watercolors of War Industry that you have up there at present," wrote Atkins to H. O. McCurry, director of the National Gallery, in 1943. "I refer to the large watercolor *Forming Bulkhead Girders*. There has been some criticism of the central figure as not conforming to a strict anatomical structure. This I purposely ignored for the following reasons.

"Art is not imitation. Life and its actions are used only as inspiration and are points of departure for the creative idea.

"Within the structure of my composition a too true rendition of the figure, recording anatomy, at any given, stop watch, [sic] moment would have produced a stilted, static appearance. Whereas by a kind of compromise between two twisted movements of the body, is seen producing the stroke. . . . The speed with which these men have to work, set up many and various poses many of them awkward and above all there is one set intent over static action—the effort to strike and strike quickly and hard the red hot girder. I think the sense of action has been successfully conveyed."

Allied artillery and air power took a fearful toll on the retreating Germans, but thousands of enemy troops, albeit disorganized and badly shaken, nevertheless lived to fight another day. Controversy has swirled ever since over exactly why the Canadians and other troops under British Field Marshal Sir Bernard Law Montgomery failed to close the gap earlier than they did, but undoubtedly the strength of German positions opposite the Canadians and the Poles had much to do with the outcome. Canada's 2nd and 3rd Infantry Divisions in Normandy suffered higher losses than any British division in the campaign, and total Canadian casualties were five thousand killed and more than thirteen thousand wounded.

German defeat in Normandy did not end the fighting in France. The First Canadian Army under General Crerar formed the coastal flank of the Allied juggernaut, moving along the English Channel into Belgium and the Netherlands. With thousands of Polish and British troops under his command, as well as three Canadian divisions and one Canadian armoured brigade and supporting troops, Crerar led the largest Canadian field army ever assembled. While Germany's armies consolidated farther to the north and east, numerous garrisons in towns and cities along the English Channel continued the fight on Hitler's orders, each one extracting its share of casualties from the Canadians. Naval gunfire sometimes persuaded the Germans that resistance was futile, but soldiers in other coastal towns fiercely stood their ground. Still, the Canadians advanced steadily,

liberating, among others, the major ports of Le Havre, Boulogne and Calais. They paused only briefly for an emotional ceremony at Dieppe, where members of the 2nd Canadian Infantry Division visited the graves of their comrades killed during the disastrous 1942 raid.

Heavy fighting, often house to house, occurring simultaneously in Italy and Northwest Europe, seriously strained Canada's personnel resources. Despite women enlisting to fill thousands of non-combat positions, vigorous recruitment efforts and repeated attempts to re-muster support troops into combat units, Canada was rapidly running out of trained infantry. As in the First World War, after the initial highly successful recruiting campaigns, volunteers became harder to find as casualty lists from overseas and well-paying jobs at home made service at the front an increasingly unattractive option. Canada's wartime labour management system likewise complicated matters, protecting thousands of workers from military service and causing friction between the three government ministers responsible for the armed services (national defence, naval services and air services) and those responsible for industrial and agricultural production. Which department should have ultimate call on scarce human resources remained a bone of contention within the Mackenzie King cabinet until the end of the war.

Many Canadians, especially those among the Progressive Conservative Opposition, blamed the difficulty in procuring troops on the National Resources Mobilization Act, which they argued shielded French

facing page:

Campbell Tinning (1910–1996)
Drifting Down, 1944
Oil on canvas
81.3 × 101.8 cm · CWM 13875

Members of the 1st Canadian Parachute Battalion training in Winterbourne Stoke, Wylye Valley, England. This unit fought as part of the 6th British Airborne Division throughout the Northwest European campaign. The peaceful scene is in marked contrast to events elsewhere. As official war artist Campbell Tinning commented in a 1979 interview: "We couldn't know what was going on all the time. We read as other people did of the disasters that were in the paper but you were only in your own little bit and it was so interesting that you hadn't time to be sad about it. Had I seen an actual bombing in London I would have, but it was always a mile away and I never saw any all the time I was there but yet heard them but there was no way I could go and see it. [Carl] Schaefer was looking out of the window when a bomb landed and he's never forgotten it. [Alex] Colville went to Belsen and he's never forgotten that naturally. They wanted me to go but they couldn't find me which is fortunate because I don't know what it would have done to me."

above:

Donald Anderson (1920–)
Dutch Refugees, 1945
Watercolour and ink on paper
38.1 × 77.6 cm · CWM 10773

Donald Anderson was an official war artist attached to the Royal Canadian Air Force. In this painting, RCAF airmen help Dutch refugees over a broken bridge outside Roermond, Holland.

Canadians from overseas service. Canadian generals, although never overly warm in defending the prime minister, had a less conspiratorial explanation: their own casualty predictions, based largely on British data from fighting in North Africa, had misjudged the extent to which the campaigns in Europe would rely primarily on infantry. As a result, they miscalculated not just the overall number of casualties Canada would suffer but also the percentage likely to occur in the infantry battalions. From the summer of 1944, Canada was in the strange position of having plenty of men and women in uniform but not nearly enough in the infantry. And infantry was urgently required at the front. Something had to be done, argued the Opposition and the generals, to reinforce depleted units on which the burden of fighting had fallen.

As early as 1942, with all three armed services and the civilian war economy expanding rapidly, Ottawa had foreseen the possibility of a future manpower crunch. The prime minister, attempting to cater to the sensibilities of both pro- and anti-conscriptionists, struck a compromise by holding a national plebiscite, not immediately to authorize compulsory overseas enlistment but merely to release the government from its earlier promise not to send conscripts abroad, should the need ever arise. The result was predictable: a solid majority of Canadians voted to free the government's hands while a solid majority of Quebec voters, 73 per cent, voted against. Most Canadians appreciated the extent to which Mackenzie King's Liberals would go to ensure

that compulsory support was not simply foisted on Quebec, as Borden's government had, in effect, done in 1917. Yet even the possibility that Ottawa would again draft men for overseas service damaged the government's standing among French-speaking Canadians and other opponents of the measure. Mackenzie King's ambiguous promise, "not necessarily conscription but conscription if necessary," has passed into the language as one of Canada's most famous political phrases, exemplifying the manoeuvres, compromises and conciliation necessary to keep Canada united in the midst of war.

At the front, the government's efforts to steer a careful middle course between supporters and opponents of compulsory service often received a more cursory hearing. As units lost trained men they could not quickly replace, or mustered in former cooks, clerks and logistics personnel to fill the gaps, the fighting power of combat units suffered along with the morale of those veterans who were left. "We had only feelings of disgust, of contempt for the prime minister and the politicians who were not facing the realities of the crisis, and most of all, we felt anger," remembered Major Joe Pigott. "The feeling was becoming very deep-seated in all the troops that they were being used and being sacrificed by their government in order not to face public opinion." With fewer replacements, or untrained ones, arriving to take up the slack, remaining veterans worked longer, harder and more often, wondering openly about the government's commitment to the war and to themselves. It was "Canada's blackest disgrace," wrote

Leonard Brooks (1911–)
Tangled Float No. 2, c. 1945
Oil on canvas
102.4 × 127.2 cm · CWM 10178

Leonard Brooks, an official war artist attached to the Royal Canadian Navy, found working at sea required flexibility. In a December 1944 letter to the director of the National Gallery, he commented: "Forgive the scrawl. We are rolling along in great style & the wardroom table gives a kick every so often. I have managed to work a system of scribbling & taking notes on this kind of rough day. By devious ways I scribble a note or two on rough paper—dodge the spray & find my way below to re-draw and fill in as much information as I can—dash up again & repeat the performance. It looks rather ridiculous—but is very effective."

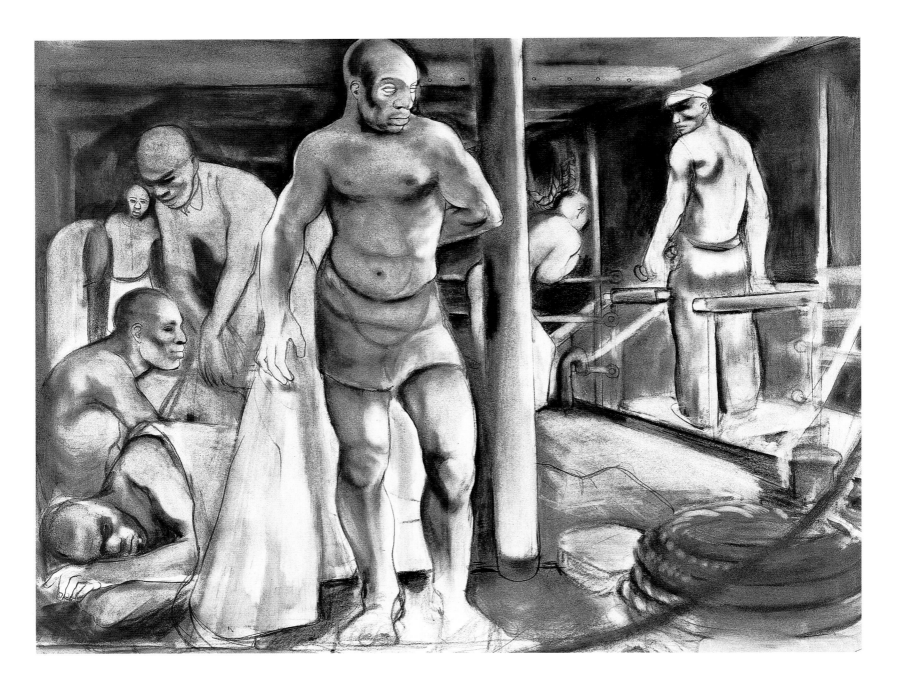

facing page:
Jack Nichols (1921–)
Negro Sailors Returning on Board a Canadian Ship, 1943
Graphite and oil washes on paper
59.2 × 73.8 cm · CWM 10522

Late in 1943, Jack Nichols was commissioned by the National Gallery of Canada to depict the activities of the Canadian Merchant Navy, the subject of this painting. On February 14, 1944, he was appointed an official war artist with the Royal Canadian Navy. He wrote to H. O. McCurry, director of the National Gallery, on August 30, 1944: "I arrived in England within a few hours of 'D' Day. Frantic efforts were made to get me on board a ship, any ship, bound for France. My materials aside from a sketch-pad were still in Scotland. In any case I managed to get aboard a Royal Navy ship assigned to a special task off the coast of France. It was a small merchant vessel, overflowing with soldiers and sailors. How I was ever wedged in is still a profound mystery to me."

left:
Official war artist Lieutenant Jack Nichols, Royal Canadian Naval Volunteer Reserve (RCNVR), on board HMCS *Iroquois* in August 1944. The zigzag stripes on his sleeves not only give his rank but also indicate the source of the RCNVR's nickname—"the wavy navy."
Artist's collection

decorated veteran Denis Whitaker. "Political games were being played with human stakes on Europe's battle-fields in October, 1944 [sic] and Canadian soldiers were the losers."

Minister of National Defence J. L. Ralston, a former colonel and First World War veteran, heard such complaints when he visited the Italian and Northwest European fronts in the fall of 1944. Returning to Canada in October, he informed the prime minister that home defence troops—the NRMA recruits, or "zombies"—would have to reinforce the units overseas—and quickly. The hard-pressed troops at the front simply could not understand the delay. A prisoner of war since the surrender of Hong Kong, Henry L. White recorded his views on the subject in a diary hidden from his Japanese captors. "In one of our Red Cross parcels was smuggled a copy of the Montreal *Gazette*, summer of '43," White noted on November 20, 1944. "They had some kind of a referendum on conscription in Canada. Apparently they are having a hard time getting recruits for active service. What the hell is the matter with those Zombies they call them. They should be here. What chance have we of ever getting out if our own people won't fight for us. Certainly a lot of bitter feeling in here over the issue."

Mackenzie King could not have known White's views, but he was not yet ready to believe his generals or his defence minister either, despite calls from the country and his own cabinet for action. Instead, he forced Ralston's resignation and appointed General McNaughton to make one last appeal for volunteers.

It failed, prompting complaints from the prime minister that he had been the victim of a "generals' revolt" to force his hand. On November 23, 1944, the government finally agreed to send NRMA conscripts overseas. In the coming months, nearly 13,000 somewhat reluctant NRMA troops went overseas, only 2463 seeing service with front-line units, where they fought well in the final months of the war. These conscripts suffered 313 casualties, 69 of them fatal.

As Allied armies moved into Belgium and northern Italy, they found not a beaten, demoralized German enemy but well-prepared defences bitterly contested at almost every turn. Italy's river valleys and vineyards, and the low-lying canals and drainage flats of coastal Belgium and Holland, were difficult obstacles for attacking troops and natural strong points for defenders. After British troops captured Antwerp in September, for example, the First Canadian Army had the unpleasant job of clearing German troops from the banks along the Scheldt estuary west of the city to permit supply ships to reach the great Belgian port.

George Blackburn and other veterans of the campaign remembered the fighting on the Scheldt in October 1944 as among the most bitter of the war. Blackburn, a member of the 4th Field Artillery Regiment, served as a forward observation officer as the Canadians pushed across flooded fields and narrow causeways to drive the Germans from the approaches to Antwerp. He paid special tribute to the infantry, on whose shoulders rested the entire operation:

Paul Goranson (1911–)
Marshalling of the Hallies, 1947
Oil on canvas
76.2 × 101.6 cm · CWM 11402

Group Captain Conn, head of Royal
Canadian Air Force historical records
during the war, wrote of Paul Goranson

in 1945: "Once when an airfield was being divebombed he continued to record
his impressions in a slit trench with
bombs bursting all around and shrapnel
flying only inches above his head."

Alex Colville (1920–)
The Nijmegen Bridge, Holland, 1946
Oil on canvas
91.5 × 122.6 cm · CWM 12187

From Alex Colville's diary: "On 12 November [1944] I returned to Nijmegen (the shelling and mortaring there is not frequent enough to be a real danger) to look for subject matter. I was unable to work because of rain, but was fascinated by the possibilities of the bridge, river and wrecked town. This silver-gray atmosphere appeals to me; the natural haziness of the atmosphere is increased by the presence of smoke generators, and the effect is beautiful."

Never dry, always covered with mud, never standing completely upright, always hunched over well below the crest of the dike he is following, never able to relax in the dread of mortar and machine-gun fire that can arrive with little or no warning as he moves crablike along its sloping side, forcing him to throw himself against the steep incline, pressing his body into the spongy wet turf as tightly as he can until they stop, or until they stop him—perhaps forever.[21]

The narrow causeways and elevated dykes not only limited the ability of German defenders to retreat from position to position but also meant that Canadian troops rarely had any other choice except frontal attack, supported by artillery and air power. Tanks, although they offered covering fire from the rear, were usually sitting ducks for German anti-tank fire on the causeways and elevated roads, leaving the main effort strictly to the infantry, engineers and artillery. Slowly, the Germans gave ground, pounded mercilessly by Canadian and Allied guns, but after four weeks of fighting the exhausted Canadians had suffered more than six thousand casualties.

After a winter respite lasting from early November to early February, the Allies renewed their advance towards Germany's Rhine River frontier along a front stretching from the Netherlands in the north to the Franco-German border in the south. By April 1945, the First Canadian Army, recently augmented by I Canadian Corps after its transfer from Italy, held the left,

or west, end of the Allied line, liberating the Netherlands and moving across northern Germany in the closing days of the war. Canadian paratroopers dropped across the Rhine with their British and American counterparts while hundreds of Canadian bombers and fighter aircraft supported the advance by blasting German cities, railroads, bridges and military installations. Germany was fast running out of reserves to reinforce its defeated armies but, as in the closing days of the First World War, individual battles were still sharp, vicious affairs. Some German garrisons and outposts surrendered willingly to Canadian troops, but many others fought almost literally to the last man. The physical and emotional cost of the fighting told heavily on Canadian troops. "I don't have the spark of my first days," remembered Charly Forbes of the Regiment de Maisonneuve. "Nothing goes well. Regardless of applying ointment on my scratches, they are easily infected. I have dreadful nightmares. . . . I have the feeling that collapse is no longer a matter of days, [but] of hours perhaps, wracked by uncontrollable shaking."[22]

The Cape Breton Highlanders, part of 11th Canadian Infantry Brigade, would remember the attack on Delfzijl, Holland, as one of its two toughest battles.[23] Attacking on April 30, 1945, the same day Adolf Hitler shot himself in his Berlin bunker, the Highlanders met a storm of artillery and small-arms fire as they advanced on the town and its nearby coastal guns. "My God," noted platoon commander Lieutenant Reg Roy in his diary, "but it was horrible to see our fellows cut up

facing page:

Edwin Holgate (1892–1977)
The Dispersal Hut, 403 Squadron,
Kenley, Surrey, c. 1944
Egg tempera on art board
61.0 × 71.2 cm · CWM 11493

A former member of the Group of
Seven, Edwin Holgate was an official
war artist with the Royal Canadian Air
Force. RCAF 403 Squadron flew Spitfires
from its base in Kenley, England. It
launched 13,004 missions between 1941
and 1945, with the loss of 85 aircraft
and 65 air and ground crew.

left:

Miller Brittain (1912–1968)
Night Target, Germany, 1946
Oil and egg tempera on Masonite
76.5 × 61.0 cm · CWM 10889

An official war artist with the Royal
Canadian Air Force, Miller Brittain
initially served as a bomb aimer.
He flew thirty-four missions and was
awarded the Distinguished Flying
Cross. "A German city under bombing,"
he said in 1957, "often looked like a
casket of jewels opening up."

Molly Lamb Bobak (1922–)

Canteen, Nijmegen, Holland, 1945

Oil and ink on canvas

51.2 × 61.1 cm · CWM 12017

The only female official war artist and a member of the Canadian Women's Army Corps, Molly Lamb Bobak was posted to Holland after V-E (Victory in Europe) Day. Her diary records the day she enlisted: "On Wednesday, the 18th of November [1942], Civilian Lamb offered herself unwillingly and willingly, willy-nilly, to the CWAC. When reporters interviewed her on Wednesday night they found her in a mental state. 'I've never known so much misery,' she stated torturedly. 'Except when I didn't win the scholarship at school. After they said my second medical was good, I was sent to different floors of the Barracks to get an arm band, a knife and fork and spoon, a mattress, 3 blankets, a pillow and two sheets. . . . I went through long dark corridors with an experienced Private who told me I must learn to walk faster and didn't answer any of my bewildered questions.'"

so . . . I hope I never see another battle like it. It was murder. . . . This has been the bitterest battle I've been in." German anti-tank guns knocked out supporting Canadian tanks while mortars and machine guns kept the Canadians pinned down along dykes and in trenches. Daylight on May 1 found hundreds of Canadians in open ground, under heavy fire and running out of ammunition. Artillery and tank support plus smoke screens and many individual acts of courage allowed the attack to press forward. After the Canadians broke through into the town, small groups of Germans began to surrender and resistance slowly petered out. The Canadians took 1520 prisoners and captured dozens of artillery pieces, anti-tank weapons and machine guns but lost twenty of their own dead and fifty-three wounded. Four days later, all German forces in Holland, Denmark and northern Germany surrendered. On May 8, Germany capitulated.

The end of the war in Europe, celebrated as V-E (Victory in Europe) Day, did not end the war. Japan continued to resist throughout the summer, despite being pounded by a relentless American strategic bombing campaign and partially starved by the tremendous success of American submarines in sinking Japanese merchant vessels. While American and Commonwealth forces advanced on several fronts across the South and Central Pacific, the United States Navy, led by a powerful fleet of aircraft carriers, swept the Imperial Japanese Navy from the sea in a series of dramatic naval engagements. Japanese ground troops continued to resist,

usually to the last man, as American infantry and marines stormed island after island, moving closer to mainland Japan, while the Japanese air force, suffering critical shortages of trained pilots, fuel and spare parts, resorted to kamikaze, or suicide, attacks against Allied warships.

At the battle of Okinawa, HMCS *Uganda*, a Canadian cruiser, helped defend American and British aircraft carriers against the desperate and devastating kamikaze raids and bombarded Japanese shore installations. In Burma, British and Indian troops inflicted a decisive defeat on the Japanese army and poured south, their offensive supported in part by two squadrons of Canadian transport aircraft. Although Ottawa was reluctant to commit large numbers of ground troops to the Pacific front, it nevertheless planned to send an infantry division, an air group and a powerful naval force (including two aircraft carriers) to join the final attack on the Japanese home islands. Two American atomic bombs, dropped on Japan in August 1945, combined with a simultaneous Russian invasion that swept Japanese forces from Manchuria in a matter of days, compelled Japan's surrender before Canada could concentrate its attention on the Pacific.

LEGACY

Canadians welcomed the end of the war with predictable emotion. "It was the Coronation, the Jubilee, the Wembley Cup and every other gathering rolled into one," wrote *The Ottawa Citizen*. Margaret Adcock watched Ste. Catherine Street in downtown Montreal fill with people on May 7 as news of Germany's impending surrender spread. "As if on cue, an army jeep came from west to east carrying four khaki-clad veterans of the 1st Division. An effigy of Hitler was lashed on the front of the vehicle. They were wildly cheered. We ran adding-machine rolls out the windows as streamers. We were notified that the building would close in half an hour. Who wanted to work anyway?"[24] Although casualties among Canada's 1.1 million military personnel had been fewer than in 1914–18 (42,000 dead and 54,000 wounded versus more than 60,000 dead and 170,000 wounded), the war still dramatically affected the country. Unlike the earlier struggle, this time Canadians had participated by the hundreds of thousands in the air and sea wars. Far more so than before, Canada's industries, ably stewarded by C. D. Howe, the minister of munitions and supply, produced vast stores of ammunition, equipment and weapons to support the Allied war effort. Canadian factories, employing hundreds of thousands of men and women, produced over 865,000 military vehicles while simultaneously producing 43,000 artillery pieces and naval guns, 16,000 aircraft of all types, over 700 warships, 3300 landing craft, 400 merchant ships and 1.8 million small arms. Numerous Crown, or state-owned, corporations helped organize the war effort, which also included more than three billion dollars in financial aid to Britain. The expertise and resources accumulated during six years of conflict, coupled with consumer spending suddenly released after years of government rationing and the scarcity of most non-essential goods, helped the economy convert relatively easily from wartime to peacetime production. Although government planners worried that unemployment and economic difficulties would plague its transition, Canada moved into the post-war world with unexpected ease.

Social scientists and academic experts helped to plan Canada's wartime economic and social programs, retrain returning military personnel and establish the foundations for Canada's post-war welfare state. Generous veterans' programs that accompanied the war (the Veterans Charter) provided an enormous infusion of people, money and interest into the country's university and vocational training system, doubling the university student population and prompting the creation of new campuses, buildings and programs. Veterans also received medical and dental care, job training, housing benefits and financial incentives that were the envy of most Western countries. Merchant navy veterans, aboriginal Canadians and women fought long, bitter and occasionally unsuccessful battles for access to the full range of government benefits, but the bulk of Canada's military personnel received generous treatment from a grateful country.

Not everyone else could say the same. Socialists, left-wing intellectuals and labour leaders demanded that benefits be extended to the rest of Canadian society to prove that the war had been fought not just to eradicate fascism but to eliminate economic inequality as well. In most Western countries, the war did herald the

Aba Bayefsky (1923–)

Perimeter Track and Dispersal at Sundown, 1945

Oil on canvas

76.7 × 96.7 cm · CWM 10874

The dark colours in this painting reflect both the time of day and the knowledge that losses are inevitable. Not all the aircraft will return from their night missions over enemy territory. An official war artist attached to the Royal Canadian Air Force, Aba Bayefsky was one of three Canadian war artists to enter Bergen-Belsen after its liberation in May 1945.

CANVAS OF WAR

facing page:

Campbell Tinning (1910–1996)
*V.J. Celebrations, Piccadilly Circus,
London,* 1945
Watercolour on paper
58.2 × 78.7 cm · CWM 14029

Victory over Japan celebrations
took place on August 15, 1945, when
that nation, having endured two atomic
bomb attacks, agreed to surrender.
Campbell Tinning remembered:
"That's exactly as it was. They're
having a hell of a good time. It was
wonderful."

left:

Charles Goldhamer (1903–1985)
Burnt Airman with Wig, 1945
Watercolour and charcoal on paper
50.1 × 39.3 cm · CWM 11237

Charles Goldhamer, an official war
artist with the Royal Canadian Air Force,
painted a series of burned airmen under-
going plastic surgery at the RCAF's plastic
surgery wing, Queen Victoria Hospital,
East Grinstead, Sussex. The clinical
detachment of the portraits owes something, perhaps, to the pastels of First
World War British plastic surgery patients
drawn by former surgeon and artist
Henry Tonks, with which Goldhamer
might well have been made familiar.

expansion of social programs and welfare benefits, but Canada demonstrated little enthusiasm for radical socialism. Borrowing carefully and selectively from the program of the leftist Co-operative Commonwealth Federation, Mackenzie King, himself a long-standing social reformer, introduced unemployment insurance in 1940 and a national family allowance program in 1944. These, combined with the initiatives dedicated specifically to veterans and their families, a national housing program and the establishment of a department of national health and welfare, represented a massive federal intrusion into the country's economic life. Although a huge expense for the treasury, they were still not the full-employment pledge demanded by socialist commentators. These programs nevertheless bolstered nicely the Liberal Party's argument during the election campaign of 1945 that it had acted not just to win the war but also to win the peace. Canadians agreed and re-elected Mackenzie King's Liberals for the third straight time.

Canada's massive military contribution earned it the right to be considered a major power by 1945, but if the government's wartime policies were any indication, there was no guarantee that post-war Ottawa might act like one. Mackenzie King's government had expressed little interest in influencing the war's strategic direction, despite its obvious effects on Canadian military efforts, and afterwards it demobilized Canada's armed forces with a speed unmatched by any of the victorious powers. This did not necessarily mean that Canada would

return to the quasi-isolationism which had marked its pre-war foreign policy, but it did mean that support for the new United Nations and other collective security efforts would be tempered by a desire to act cautiously and in concert with like-minded states. A new foreign policy term—functionalism—even emerged to describe Canada's diplomatic strategy, meaning to act boldly only in areas of direct concern to vital Canadian interests.

Some Canadian soldiers and diplomats were prepared, even in 1945, to go much further. Having just weathered another conscription debate due to overseas military commitments, the Mackenzie King government was unlikely to do more, barring dramatic changes in the international environment. Within Canada's foreign service, a new activism had emerged, but it had not captured the prime minister. In early 1948, after a Communist *coup d'état* in Czechoslovakia, Mackenzie King nevertheless consented to secret security discussions with the United States and Britain, which led, ultimately, to the formation of the North Atlantic Treaty Organization the following year.

As in 1918, however, in 1945 the future state of Canada's social welfare system or foreign policy concerned most Canadians very little. Beginning in May, the first of more than 750,000 military personnel then in uniform began to return to civilian life and long-awaited reunions with families and friends. Much had happened in their absence. Most families had survived the war intact, but many had not. Many new ones,

including thousands of marriages between Canadian service personnel and European spouses, had been created. All hoped that post-war Canada would match the flowery election rhetoric of June 1945, but many, especially those who had lived through the interwar period, bore a healthy scepticism towards official promises of a better world to come. Canadians who had liberated the Nazi death camps, endured treatment as prisoners of war by Imperial Japan or simply survived the brutal air, sea and ground campaigns in Europe, the North Atlantic and the Pacific, needed no lessons on the depths of human depravity. Twice in a generation Canadians had marched off to war, and the second time, as everyone now knew, they had helped save the world from unprecedented evil. Canadians embraced the post-war period, grateful that their country had been spared the ravages of invasion, occupation or mass bombing, but aware too that in the face of some future threat their efforts might again be needed to fight aggressors in a common cause. The country eased into the post-war world a proud, confident democracy made secure by the sacrifices of its citizens-in-arms.

facing page:

Tony Law (1916–1996)

Corvettes Sailing up the St. Lawrence to the Graveyard, c. 1945
Oil on canvas
56.0 × 66.5 cm · CWM 10253

One hundred twenty-two corvettes, most of them built in Canada, formed the bulk of the Royal Canadian Navy's anti-submarine fleet and were an important part of the Allied war effort. Designed for service in coastal waters, these little ships were all that was available to meet the concerted German submarine attacks on merchant ship convoys when the battle for the seas was in the balance from 1941 to 1943.

Tony Law recalled making this painting: "I went wild with the skies . . . and then had the cloud patterns on the water and the sun breaking between the clouds making a pattern [and] design. Of course, I was brought up on the St. Lawrence in Quebec so I knew [it] well because I had my own little sailboat. I used to sail up and down . . . and paint and then war broke out and ended it all."

page 151:

Jack Nichols (1921–)

Normandy Scene, Beach in Gold Area, 1946
Oil on canvas
123.2 × 138.4 cm · CWM 10523

Jack Nichols witnessed the dislocation that followed the successful invasion of Normandy on June 6, 1944. The piece of driftwood in the foreground signifies the loss of life in a sector that had been assaulted by British troops.

page 154:

Alex Colville (1920–)

Bodies in a Grave, Belsen, 1946
Oil on canvas
76.3 × 101.6 cm · CWM 12122

In May 1945, official war artists Alex Colville, Donald Anderson and Aba Bayefsky entered Bergen-Belsen shortly after its liberation. Colville noted: "This being in Bergen-Belsen was strange. As I've said to a number of people, the thing one felt was one felt badly that one didn't feel worse. That is to say, you see one dead person and it is too bad, but seeing five hundred is not five hundred times worse. There is a certain point at which you begin to feel nothing. . . . It was a profoundly affecting experience. Obviously it would be, unless a person was an absolute fool. You were bound to think about this quite a bit."

ENDNOTES

1 J. W. Pickersgill, *The Mackenzie King Record, Volume 1: 1939–1944* (Toronto: University of Toronto Press, 1960), p 39.

2 J. L. Granatstein, *Canada's War: The Politics of the Mackenzie King Government, 1939–1945* (Toronto: Oxford University Press, 1975), pp 19–20.

3 Howard Graham, *Citizen and Soldier: The Memoirs of Lieutenant-General Howard Graham* (Toronto: McClelland & Stewart, 1987), pp 108–9.

4 Herb Peppard, *The LightHearted Soldier: A Canadian's Exploits with the Black Devils in World War II* (Halifax: Nimbus Publishing, 1994), p 7.

5 Cited in Bill McNeil, *Voices of a War Remembered: An Oral History of Canadians in World War II* (Toronto: Doubleday Canada, 1991), p 42.

6 Basil Bartlett, *My First War: An Army Officer's Journal for May 1940, through Belgium to Dunkirk* (London: Chatto & Windus, 1940), p 115.

7 Cited in Bill McNeil, *Voices of a War Remembered*, p 142.

8 Cited in Ted Barris and Alex Barris, *Days of Victory: Canadians Remember, 1939–1945* (Toronto: Macmillan Canada, 1995), pp 64–5.

9 Ibid., p 67.

10 Bill McNeil, *Voices of a War Remembered*, p 101.

11 Barris and Barris, *Days of Victory*, p 39.

12 Cited in C. P. Stacey and Barbara M. Wilson, *The Half-Million: The Canadians in Britain, 1939–1946* (Toronto: University of Toronto Press, 1987), p 37.

13 Denis Whitaker and Shelagh Whitaker, *Dieppe: Tragedy to Triumph* (Toronto: McGraw-Hill Ryerson, 1992), pp 76–77.

14 Barry Broadfoot, *Six War Years, 1939–1945: Memories of Canadians at Home and Abroad* (Toronto: Doubleday, 1974), p 134.

15 Whitaker and Whitaker, *Dieppe: Tragedy to Triumph*, p 243.

16 Cited in Whitaker and Whitaker, *Dieppe: Tragedy to Triumph*, p 247.

17 Strome Galloway, *Bravely into Battle: The Autobiography of a Canadian Soldier in World War II* (Toronto: Stoddart, 1988 [1981]), p 168.

18 Charles Cromwell Martin (with Roy Whitsed), *Battle Diary: From D-Day and Normandy to the Zuider Zee and VE* (Toronto: Dundurn Press, 1994), p 6.

19 Cited in Bill McAndrew et al., *Normandy 1944: The Canadian Summer* (Montreal: Art Global, 1994), p 80.

20 Martin, *Battle Diary*, p 67.

21 George G. Blackburn, *The Guns of Victory: A Soldier's Eye View, Belgium, Holland, and Germany, 1944–45* (Toronto: McClelland & Stewart, 1996), p 128.

22 Charly Forbes, *Fantassin: Pour mon pays, la gloire et . . . des prunes* (Sillery: Septendrion, 1994), pp 185–86.

23 The citations on Delfzijl are from Alex Morrison and Ted Slaney, *The Breed of Manly Men: The History of the Cape Breton Highlanders* (Toronto: Canadian Institute of Strategic Studies and The Cape Breton Highlanders Association, 1994), pp 311–32.

24 Barris and Barris, *Days of Victory*, pp 208–9.

THE ART OF TOTAL WAR

It is logical that artists should be a part of the organization of total war, whether to provide inspiration, information or comment on the glory or the stupidity of war.

A.Y. JACKSON

THE SECOND WORLD WAR produced a markedly different Canadian art program and a less splendid public launch from the Canadian War Memorials of the First World War. In September 1946, the art of Canada at war was not unveiled in the imperial splendour of Burlington House, London, but in the cramped and somewhat dingy premises of the National Gallery of Canada, in the Victoria Memorial Building in Ottawa. Because the program had been seen from the beginning as a distinctly national effort, it was fitting that its first major public showing should be in the nation's capital.

For most Canadians, the First World War was a human tragedy of vast dimensions barely redeemed by the perceived rightness of its cause. The Second World War was different. This conflict was viewed clearly as a just war, which had to be fought to preserve freedom and democracy. It was an attitude that survived in the face of the tremendous loss of human life, the massive dislocation of peoples and a myriad of previously unimaginable atrocities.

The Second World War art scheme shared this outlook, and a majority of its paintings portray a positive war. There are no huge memorial compositions focussing on destruction, tragedy and misery. Instead, most of the more than five thousand small paintings record the locations, events, machinery and personnel of wartime on all fronts, in an often depersonalized manner.

However, like the Canadian War Memorials, the Second World War effort depended on the energies of a committed few. The most important player was Canada's High Commissioner to Great Britain, Vincent Massey. He came from a well-to-do family that owned the Massey-Harris farm-machinery manufacturing company, and he had always been interested in the arts. Small in stature but given to self-importance, Massey was a collector of Canadian art, and he proved critical to the success of the Canadian war art program.

Massey's office was at Canada House on Trafalgar Square, London, a stone's throw from the British National Gallery and its director, Kenneth Clark. Massey also collected British art, and in 1941 he became a trustee—and in 1943 chairman—of the board of trustees of Britain's National Gallery. By virtue of his position and his interests, he moved easily in Clark's circle. Massey was familiar with Canada's First World War art (he was an early supporter of war artist David Milne), and probably Clark spoke of the deep impression the collection had made on him in 1919. Certainly, in response to the success of the Canadian War Memorials, and the subsequent British undertaking, Clark was swift to launch a similar plan in Britain during the

Jack Humphrey (1901–1967)

A Canadian Sailor, c. 1942
Oil on canvas
76.1 × 61.0 cm · CWM 4568

The circumstances of the creation of this work, before any official war art commission, demonstrate the remarkable dedication that produced Canada's Second World War art collection. The First World War artist A.Y. Jackson suggested that Jack Humphrey undertake the painting. The National Gallery then had no funds with which to acquire the painting and was able to do so only with the assistance of an anonymous donor.

157

Left to right: Official war artist Carl Schaefer, Sir Kenneth Clark, director of England's National Gallery, the Duchess of Kent and Canadian High Commissioner Vincent Massey at the opening of the Canadian war artists exhibition at the National Gallery, London, England, February 9, 1944.

Department of National Defence PL 22848

Second World War. Massey wanted to follow suit with a Canadian project, but Clark had an emotional advantage: the fact that Britain was was coming under German air attack. Clark was able to harness the idea of war art to the need for propaganda. War art would help save Britain.

Massey could not make the same argument. To most Canadians in 1939, the war posed no immediate threat. It was simply too far away. As well, given their lamentable state of preparedness, the Canadian military services had the greater issues of personnel and *matériel* to deal with. Recruitment, training, supplies, logistics and "doing their bit" for Britain were of paramount importance. Furthermore, unlike Massey, most Canadians, including the military, were unfamiliar with the First World War art because most of the works had been kept in storage at the National Gallery of Canada since 1921. The few reproductions issued to schools after the war by the Imperial Order Daughters of the Empire had been denounced as warmongering, and they had therefore remained largely uncirculated. The First World War art collection was already Canada's hidden treasure.

Some of the first works by British war artists were exhibited at Britain's National Gallery as early as December 1939. Immediately, Massey suggested that Canada set up a program of its own. Defence officials in Ottawa initially responded with indifference. Meanwhile, in Ottawa, H. O. McCurry, Eric Brown's successor as director of the National Gallery, had begun his own lobbying effort. Throughout the war, he ensured that examples of Canada's First World War art hung in a gallery set aside specifically for that purpose. Given that the National Gallery was at the time sharing premises with two other museums, this action was no mean feat. McCurry had the support of the trustees of the National Gallery who included in their 1939–40 report a motion that the Second World War be recorded by Canadian artists.

Despite Massey and McCurry's initial lack of success in establishing a full-fledged endeavour, they did make progress, and Canadians were soon producing paintings depicting the war effort. A number of artists had enlisted in the armed forces and, inspired by their knowledge of the Canadian War Memorials, contacted McCurry to suggest they would be more useful as artists in uniform than as foot soldiers. McCurry in turn passed their offers to National Defence Headquarters. There, the rigorously formal yet far-seeing Colonel A. F. Duguid, director of the historical section of the general staff, employed Private E. J. Hughes and Sapper O. N. Fisher to depict activities in the army. In England, Massey arranged for Trooper W. A. Ogilvie to be attached to Canadian military headquarters as an artist.

In late 1940, when Major C. P. Stacey was appointed as the Canadian Army's historical officer in London, Massey and McCurry acquired a major ally. One of Stacey's first tasks was to coordinate the itinerary of the notable English artist Henry Lamb, who as a British war artist had undertaken in 1941 to paint the Canadian Army in England. Early in 1942, Stacey also helped to formalize the hiring of Hughes, Fisher and Ogilvie and

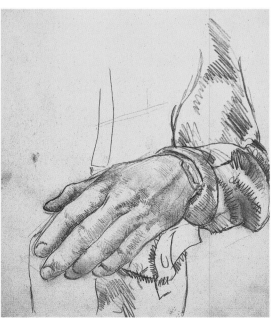

Alex Colville (1920–)

Infantry, near Nijmegen, Holland, 1946
Oil on canvas
101.6 × 121.9 cm · CWM 12172

Infantry, 1945
Carbon pencil on paper
22.9 × 19.1 cm · CWM 12145.6

Hand Study, 1945
Carbon pencil on paper
25.4 × 20.3 cm · CWM 82370

The practice of sketching was common to all the war artists, but the work of Alex Colville is unique in that extensive preliminary work for so many of his paintings has survived. Sometimes the finished painting is extremely close to the original drawing, whereas at other times the sketches form the basis for only a small detail in a picture. Taken together, however, Colville's drawings provide a special opportunity to understand the creative process behind a painting of war.

Colville noted in his diary: "Painting in cold weather presents several problems. On the average winter day I find it impossible to work outside for more than an hour at a time as after that my hands are numb. Watercolours will not dry outdoors, and sometimes even freezes [sic] on the paper or in the pans. One solution to these problems is to drive the jeep to a selected point of view and paint from inside the vehicle, warming the interior with an oil heater. Another, in places where the jeep cannot be taken, is to paint outdoors, but to go into a dugout or house at intervals to dry washes before a stove. A third solution is to make quick drawings on the spot and paint large works in billets from these sketches. At present I find this last method most satisfactory."

There are seventeen sketches in the Canadian War Museum associated with *Infantry, near Nijmegen, Holland,* the moving canvas depicting soldiers of the 3rd Canadian Infantry Division trudging along a Dutch polder. The preliminary drawings show that Colville worked on uniform details and on specific parts of the soldiers' stances and anatomy. He worked with two concepts for the finished painting, however. One features the figures moving towards the viewer, and the other, away. The only completed watercolour is of the latter, which suggests that the final composition was not the one the artist initially chose to develop.

Colville himself was brief in a diary description of how the composition came into being: "On 1 February [1945] I envisaged my first big canvas—the subject being infantry marching in single file along a road. That morning I made numerous sketches of the Royal Winnipeg Rifles marching, then a study of a desolate road. The following day . . . I did a pen and wash drawing, *Infantry,* from the previous day's sketches."

to obtain for them commissions as officers with the rank of second lieutenant. A methodical, extraordinarily well-organized man and, ultimately, one of Canada's most influential military historians, Stacey got the army's art program going. Its success, which led the air force and the navy to follow suit, played a significant role in the eventual formation of the Canadian War Records.

In Canada, artists such as A.Y. Jackson, a member of the Group of Seven and one of the earliest of Canada's First World War painters, were also lobbying for a war art program. Another domestic catalyst was a growing public awareness that artists had a role to play in society; if war was an important expression of society, then they should record it. The developing sense of nationalism undoubtedly contributed to the mounting pressure for an artistic war record as well. Because Canada had entered the Second World War as an independent nation, Canadian artists should capture on canvas the country's achievements in battle.

Despite the initiatives of Massey, McCurry, Duguid and Stacey, not to mention the Canadian art establishment as a whole, the first four years of the war were only minimally recorded. In fact, there was a setback, as Stacey recorded in his memoirs: "At the beginning of April 1942, . . . we were told that Fisher, whose imminent dispatch had been announced, would not be coming, no more artists would be sent, and the appointment of Mrs. Lilias Newton, whom Massey had asked for as a portrait artist, was rejected." The continued lack of support meant there would be no eyewitness paintings of

the fall of Hong Kong in 1941 or of the Dieppe Raid in 1942. Indeed, the bulk of the work produced by Lamb, Hughes and Ogilvie in this period was restricted to depicting training exercises in Great Britain.

In October 1942, Stacey's unauthorized and "slightly illegal program" added Lieutenant L. P. Harris, the son of celebrated Group of Seven painter Lawren S. Harris. However, the less-than-enthusiastic response of the colour-blind Minister of National Defence, Colonel J. L. Ralston, to the art completed to date did not bode well for the project's future. Nonetheless, late in 1942, the indefatigable Massey again tried to have an official war art program put in place. This time his request made it through the bureaucracy to Prime Minister Mackenzie King's desk. Perhaps Ralston had not been as lukewarm as Stacey had thought. In an interesting *volte-face* from his circumspect attitude to the art of the First World War, Mackenzie King agreed to the official employment of war artists.

Formally set up in January 1943, a committee consisting of McCurry and senior military personnel from the army, air force and navy ran the program in Canada and selected the artists. The lobbying effort had resulted in a substantial pool of names from which they could draw. The two main criteria were service experience and artistic ability. In Britain, Massey was the guiding light while senior officers in the services handled the mechanics. Stacey, for example, continued to direct the work of the army's artists. Even a cursory look at his files in the National Archives of Canada reveals

Official war artists attached to the Canadian Army, 1946. Standing from left to right are: Orville Fisher, George Pepper, Will Ogilvie, E. J. Hughes, Molly Lamb Bobak, Charles Comfort, George Stanley (historian), Alex Colville, Campbell Tinning and Bruno Bobak. Seated, left to right: National Gallery director H. O. McCurry and painter A.Y. Jackson. The painting behind them is *A Canadian Gun Pit* by Wyndham Lewis, a First World War painting now in the collection of the National Gallery of Canada.

National Gallery of Canada

facing page:

Charles Comfort (1900–1994)
Campobasso, c. 1945
Oil on canvas
127.5 × 153.2 cm · CWM 12244

From Charles Comfort's diary: "It was still quite dark when [a colleague] roused us at 0445 hours on that last morning in Campobasso. The movement order had been circulated and we knew officially the route we would follow that day to reach the first staging camp, designated as Petacciato. The approach march to the battle-line was to take possibly three days, then once committed we would strike hard and fast towards Pescara. We were on the move again, racing towards the grimmest action of the campaign. Happily we were innocent of that fact, and spirits ran high as we sighted the blue waters of the Adriatic from above Casacalenda, and far out on the horizon the Tremiti islands, shimmering in the sunshine."

left:

Charles Comfort (1900–1994)
Self-portrait (Major C. F. Comfort), 1944
Watercolour on paper
51.4 × 34.3 cm · CWM 12265

On June 16, 1944, Charles Comfort wrote in his diary from Piedimonte d'Alife: "I did this in a huge mirror borrowed from the Rear by the sergeant. As a result the portrait is, of course, in reverse."

Official war artist Charles Comfort painting *Battlefield near Berardi Cross Roads.* This critical battle, in which the Royal 22nd Regiment distinguished itself, took place outside Ortona, Italy, in December 1943.
National Archives of Canada 30869

what a huge undertaking it proved to be. There are hundreds of letters from people requesting work as official war artists, hundreds of notes regarding the movements of painters and dossier after dossier of war art listings, including records of when images were photographed and requests for their use.

Those hired as official war artists, ultimately thirty-one officers, were given rank, pay, supplies and instructions. They were divided approximately evenly between the three services. The army was quick to engage painters and had initially the most artists in the field, followed by the air force. The navy remained the least organized of the three services at producing war art, although it may, ultimately, have employed more innovative painters. Only one woman artist was hired. A.Y. Jackson recommended twenty-three-year-old Molly Lamb, a junior officer in the Canadian Women's Army Corps. However, unlike her male colleagues, she was not allowed overseas until after the war in Europe ended, in May 1945.

The instructions that the artists received suggest that they had little room to manoeuvre artistically. Their directions specified the size and quantity of their paintings as well as the subjects:

You are expected to record and interpret vividly and veraciously, according to your artistic sense, (1) the spirit and character, the appearance and attitude of the men, as individuals or groups, of the Service to which you are attached—(2) the instruments and machines which they employ, and (3) the environment in which they do their work. The intention is that your productions shall be worthy of Canada's highest cultural traditions, doing justice to History, and as works of art, worthy of exhibition anywhere at any time.

Accuracy was paramount, and the degree to which the artists saw this precision as important can be seen in the thousands of small sketches completed of equipment, vehicles, uniforms and machines.

The work order followed by most war artists differed very little from that of their First World War predecessors. They had all been trained in a traditional way of working largely unchanged from the late eighteenth century. Sketchbooks were critical. Those of official army artist Orville Fisher were unusually creative. In preparation for the D-Day invasion on June 6, 1944, he made tiny waterproof pads of paper that he strapped to his wrist. That day, he leaped from his landing craft, raced up the beach and, once relatively safe, made rapid, on-the-spot sketches of the actions. He never drew people accurately but resorted to simple stick figures, knowing that he could develop them later.

Larger watercolours were painted in the field but away from battle. The time, date, location, event or the names of the units depicted were carefully noted on the back. Historical officers attached to the same units as the artists assessed these compositions for accuracy and for any breach of censorship before the pieces were forwarded to London. Once the war in Europe was over, the artists were sent back to Canada, where they were provided with studio space to complete a predetermined number of canvasses based on these watercolours.

Most artists were sensitive to the dead. One soldier noted that army artist Charles Comfort had carefully covered the face of a dead German who lay, unburied, close to the painter's selected subject. Although naval artist Harold Beament painted a burial at sea, he was so concerned that depressing images might adversely affect morale that he avoided them. Jack Nichols, another naval artist, had no such compunction and, in one of the most wrenching images of the war, depicted a drowning German sailor. For the most part, however, the war artists were not truly prepared for the subject matter that awaited them. Largely trained in a landscape painting tradition, they were poorly equipped to deal pictorially with the reality of war. Thus, Comfort's dramatic painting of Campobasso, Italy, says more about his appreciation for the landscapes of Renaissance artist Giovanni Bellini than it does for his interest in the Canadian army.

The home front and the work of women in particular were neglected initially. McCurry recognized this, but not until 1944 did he hire artists such as Pegi Nicol MacLeod to paint the women's services in Ottawa. MacLeod exemplified both the artist who wanted to paint the war and the artist who could record it in a manner not constrained by the official instructions. She produced exuberant watercolours of service women dating from 1944 and 1945, shortly after a symbolic series of

paintings of her daughter Jane for whose future, and that of all other children, she considered the war was being fought. Several of her paintings combine the elements of child, mother, victory parade and homecoming, to convey what the women left behind felt the war to be about.

All through the war, impromptu and formal exhibitions of Canadian war art were organized in Canada, in continental Europe and in Britain. The services also offered art classes and art competitions for servicemen and women. Art was popular, and there were huge numbers of requests for reproductions of official war art.

Although the Second World War art program was an undoubted success, like the Canadian War Memorials, what to do with the works once the war was over became an issue. By cabinet decree, the Second World War Canadian War Records were deposited with the National Gallery in 1946, but a curator was not appointed until 1960. Until the collection was transferred to the Canadian War Museum in 1971, the curator selected works for changing exhibits in a designated gallery space. In part because the war museum has been able to show only a limited number of the works, both war art collections are known only to a privileged few. Nonetheless, the paintings powerfully commemorate the conflicts from the perspective of those who witnessed them. Although to a certain extent the paintings illustrate the war's events, the works also convey the feelings of those who were there. This personal experience of war is perhaps, as those who recall the wars die, the art programs' most important legacy.

Pegi Nicol MacLeod (1904–1949)
Salmon in the Galley, 1944
Oil on canvas
76.2 × 91.7 cm · CWM 14215

In the late summer of 1944, the National Gallery of Canada commissioned Pegi Nicol MacLeod to paint the women's services in Ottawa. In the December 1944 issue of *Canadian Art*, she described her experience painting in the barracks of the Women's Royal Canadian Naval Service (WRCNS): "When we come to the kitchens and galleys where the foods are prepared for these war-changed girls, we arrive at a group of animated Brueghels . . . there was cerulean blue for the W.R.C.N. [sic] stewards dealing with yard-square pans of stews and custards, baskets of cutlets, of sea salmon, silver and vermillion. . . . Here in the galleys life was joyous with the girls singing, amazingly agreeable under their hanging pots and sieves."

EPILOGUE

CANADA AT THE END of the millennium, with over thirty million citizens, maintains merely sixty thousand men and women in its regular armed forces, and another thirty thousand in the reserves. They are small numbers, even for a nation at peace. Despite the power of television to shock us daily with brutal images of conflict around the globe, war resides for most Canadians on the margins of memory, far removed from their living rooms and playgrounds. It is a phenomenon to be observed or marvelled at when it appears on the CBC *National* perhaps, but not one to be studied, remembered or learned from. Serried ranks of veterans parading on November 11 are a recurrent but fading feature of the cultural montage. Young Canadians know Wayne Gretzky or Shania Twain, not Billy Bishop or Mackenzie King. If the heritage of war reverberates at all in the collective conscience, it is a low, distant echo, inaudible to all but the keenest few. National surveys remind us repeatedly that Canadians are ignorant of their history. The disservice visited by the present on the past is broad, deep and unconscionable.

Perhaps it was always this way. Just as war-weariness led Canadians after 1918, and again after 1945, to bring home their armies and demobilize their troops, so too did the war artists retreat into the pages of books and the walls of museums and galleries. Largely disarmed when war broke out on the Korean Peninsula in 1950, Canada reluctantly sent troops and warships but no artists. The ambitious programs had always needed a champion— a Lord Beaverbrook or a Vincent Massey pulling strings to realize their personal, national visions—but in 1950 there was none. Not until 1968 would the war art collections' then curator, R. F. Wodehouse, initiate the Canadian Armed Forces Civilian Artists' Program (CAFCAP), to depict the activities of Canada's military at home and abroad. The program, which never replicated the success of its forebears in attracting the best talent, fell victim to budget cuts in 1995. In 1994, only the intervention of an infantry battalion's commanding officer, about to head to Croatia for United Nations peacekeeping duty, assured that a war artist went along, his passage paid by funds raised from the unit's members. The CAFCAP initiative carved out a precarious niche in Canada's Cold War military, but it would have no post–Cold War successor.

It is a shame. The art produced by Canada's two official programs offers a mesmerizing glance at the face of war. Produced under often difficult conditions by some of the country's finest artists, the works constitute a unique visual record of the country's horrific, heroic past. Like all great art, they speak to the spirit of their times, to the battles lost and won, to the lives consumed in fire and to the shattered families left behind to rebuild. They speak democratically, silently, to all Canadians, not of any nationalist mythology or maudlin sentiment but simply of the experience of generations, now passing, whose sacrifices formed the foundation of modern Canada. We have tried to tell both stories here: the history of a people at war and of the artists who painted them.

Jack Nichols (1921–)
Drowning Sailor, 1946
Oil on canvas
76.2 × 61.0 cm · CWM 10505

The Royal Canadian Navy grew from only six seagoing warships and 3500 personnel in September 1939 to over 100,000 men and women and some 300 seagoing warships by the end of 1944. During the course of the war, the Canadian navy sank or helped destroy 32 enemy submarines and several surface warships. The navy's losses included 2024 personnel killed or died on service and 24 warships. Describing this painting in a 1998 interview, Jack Nichols commented: "When you are drowning you lose your nationality, don't you?"

CHRONOLOGY

FIRST WORLD WAR

August 1914 First World War begins

October 1914 Canada's First Contingent arrives in Britain

April 1915 Second Battle of Ypres, Canada's first major battle

September 1916 Canadian Corps joins the Battle of the Somme

November 1916 Canadian War Memorials Fund officially registered as a charity in London, England

April 1917 Canadians capture Vimy Ridge

June 1917 Sir Arthur Currie becomes the first (and only) Canadian to command the Canadian Corps

August 1917 Military Service Act, providing for conscription for overseas service, becomes law

October 1917 Canadians attack Passchendaele Ridge, finally capturing their objectives the following month

December 1917 Federal election returns a Union Government, which pledges to support conscription and a maximum war effort

March 1918 Canada's first war artists, Fred Varley, Maurice Cullen, William Beatty and Charles Simpson, leave Canada for the United Kingdom

August 1918 Canadian Corps spearheads Allied attack at Amiens at the start of the Hundred Days

November 1918 First World War ends

December 1920 Canadian War Memorials Fund art collection given to Canada and placed in the custody of the National Gallery of Canada

SECOND WORLD WAR

September 1939 German invasion of Poland marks the start of the Second World War; Canada declares war on September 10

September 1939 First transatlantic merchant ship convoy departs from Halifax

December 1939 1st Canadian Infantry Division arrives in England

December 1939	Canada and other countries sign the British Commonwealth Air Training Plan agreement
June 1940	Ottawa passes the National Resources Mobilization Act
August 1940	United States and Canada agree to a Permanent Joint Board on Defence
July 1941	Women's Auxiliary Air Force—later the Royal Canadian Air Force (Women's Division)—and the Canadian Women's Army Corps created (the Women's Royal Canadian Naval Service follows in July 1942)
December 1941	Canadian troops helping to defend Hong Kong are defeated and captured by Japanese forces
August 1942	Canadian troops suffer defeat in a raid on Dieppe on the French coast of the English Channel
January 1943	Canadian War Records art scheme receives cabinet approval
January 1943	No. 6 (Royal Canadian Air Force) Group, the war's largest Canadian air formation, established in Bomber Command
April 1943	Rear-Admiral L. W. Murray, the only Canadian theatre commander of the war, heads Canadian Northwest Atlantic theatre
July 1943	Canadian troops participate in the Allied invasion of Sicily
September 1943	Canadian troops participate in the Allied invasion of the Italian mainland
December 1943	Battle of Ortona, Italy
June 1944	Allies invade France at several points along the Normandy coast—one of five invasion beaches is assigned to the Canadian Army
November 1944	Canadian government agrees to send conscript troops overseas
May 1945	Germany surrenders
August 1945	Japan surrenders, ending the Second World War
September 1946	Canadian War Records collection given to National Gallery of Canada
October 1971	Canadian War Memorials and Canadian War Records collections transferred to the Canadian War Museum

SOURCES

THIS BOOK IS INDEBTED to a variety of primary and secondary sources. For information on the artists, their paintings and the programs in which they took part, we have relied particularly heavily on collections at the National Archives of Canada, the National Gallery of Canada and the Canadian War Museum. We also used war artist files at the Imperial War Museum, London, and the Beaverbrook papers at the House of Lords Record Office. Unless otherwise noted, all quotations and personal anecdotes from the war years recounted in chapters one and three come from personal records in the Canadian War Museum's archives.

Our background material included general histories, biographies, battle studies and personal memoirs, many of them gleaned from O. A. Cooke, *The Canadian Military Experience 1867–1995: A Bibliography* (1997). Official histories were an essential starting point. G. W. L. Nicholson, *Canadian Expeditionary Force, 1914–1919* (1962) and S. F. Wise, *Canadian Airmen and the First World War* (1980), we used frequently. For the 1940s, C. P. Stacey, *Arms, Men and Governments: The War Policies of Canada, 1939–1945* (1970) was the starting point. Two volumes of Canadian Army history—Nicholson's volume two, *The Canadians in Italy, 1943–1945* (1956) and Stacey's volume three, *The Victory Campaign: Operations in North West Europe, 1944–1945* (1960)—were especially helpful. W. A. B.

Douglas, *The Creation of a National Air Force* (1986) and Brereton Greenhous et al., *The Crucible of War, 1939–1945* (1994) for the air force, Joseph Schull, *The Far Distant Ships* (1950) and Gilbert Norman Tucker, *The Naval Service of Canada* (1952) for the navy, were vital.

General histories provided a narrative backbone, including two by J. L. Granatstein and Desmond Morton, *A Nation Forged in Fire: Canadians and the Second World War, 1939–1945* (1989) and *Marching to Armageddon: Canadians and the Great War, 1914–1919* (1989). Granatstein's *Canada's War: The Politics of the Mackenzie King Government, 1939–1945* (1975) remains the standard text; Morton's *When Your Number's Up: The Canadian Soldier in the First World War* (1993) is equally definitive. Daphne Read (ed.), *The Great War and Canadian Society: An Oral History* (1978), Will Bird, *Ghosts Have Warm Hands* (1968) and Reginald H. Roy (ed.), *The Journal of Private Fraser* (1998) provided detail and colour for the first war. Ruth Roach Pierson, *"They're Still Women after All": The Second World War and Canadian Womanhood* (1986), Spencer Dunmore, *Wings for Victory* (1994) and two volumes by Marc Milner, *North Atlantic Run* (1985) and *The U-Boat Hunters* (1994), did the same for the second.

While extremely helpful, the published literature on the history of the war art programs is neither extensive nor exhaustive. Heather Robertson's exhibition catalogue, *A Terrible Beauty: The Art of Canada at War* (1977), is a classic, and two journals, *Canadian Military History* and *Legion*, publish regular war art features.

Maria Tippett, *Art at the Service of War* (1984), is a thorough account of the First World War program, but there is no Second World War equivalent. Joan Murray, *Canadian Artists of the Second World War* (1981), provides only a brief overview, but her interviews with war artists, now in the National Archives of Canada, are critical. Many artists featured in this book have published diaries, letters or memoirs, including A.Y. Jackson, Charles Comfort, Tony Law, Alex Colville, Molly Lamb Bobak and a significant number of the British First World War artists. Material from these volumes has been quoted in the captions in particular. C. P. Stacey's autobiography, *A Date with History* (1983), is also very helpful on the Second World War army art program. Charles C. Hill's *The Group of Seven: Art for a Nation* (1995) provides especially useful insight into the Canadian First World War art program. Further references to war artists' experiences can be found in a number of published catalogues and newspaper or journal articles. They can also be found in unpublished theses and articles specific to particular artists' careers as a whole.

overleaf:

Alfred Bastien (1873–1955)
Over the Top, Neuville-Vitasse, 1918
Detail · entire image shown on p. 47
Oil on canvas
140.5 × 229.6 cm · CWM 8058

INDEX OF ARTISTS